IN THE SW

MORECAMBE'S SUPER SWIMMING STADIUM

BARRY AND LESLEY GUISE

"Here was no ordinary lido. Here was an unashamed swimming stadium, and a Super Swimming Stadium at that. As an architectural statement, Kenneth Cross and Cecil Sutton's colossal creation dwarfed any of its contemporaries, and might even be considered the greatest of them all."

Janet Smith (*Liquid Assets: The Lidos and Open Air Swimming Pools of Britain*)

First published in 2022

by Broadlands Press

Copyright © Barry and Lesley Guise

All rights reserved
Unauthorised duplication contravenes existing laws

The right of Barry and Lesley Guise to be identified as the authors of this work has been asserted in accordance with the Copyright, Designs and Patents act 1988

British Library Cataloguing-in-Publication data
A catalogue record for this book is available from the British Library

Paperback ISBN 13: 978-1-3999-1992-0

Designed and typeset by Carnegie Book Production
www.carnegiebookproduction.com

Printed and bound by Severn

CONTENTS

1	TAKING THE PLUNGE	4
2	THE BEST LAID PLANS …	22
3	HEALTH ABOUNDS	34
4	PEACE AND WAR	50
5	LOONIES AND LOVELIES	70
	STADIUM SNIPPETS	101
6	BEAUTY SURROUNDS	112
7	FAREWELL MY LIDO	158
8	GREAT EXPECTATIONS AND HARD TIMES	166
9	THIS OTHER EDEN	182
	Acknowledgements	188
	Authors	188
	Bibliography	189
	Image credits	190
	Index	191

TAKING THE PLUNGE

ONE

Nowadays we take for granted the simple pleasures of swimming in a pool or splashing around in the sea while on holiday but, for the British at least, these are relatively modern notions. While children through the ages played happily in any small puddle they could find, adults were more concerned with the necessities of life; water was for drinking – but only if fresh and clean – while rivers, lakes and the sea could provide a welcome, if unpredictable, source of food.

As societies developed so did attitudes to water based activities; even washing started to find favour. When the Romans arrived in Britain they constructed, in places such as Bath, bathing pools large enough for swimming but whose primary purpose was hygiene and health. It is said that Roman soldiers were expected to be able to swim (in armour!) but this was probably no more than the ability to scramble ashore from a boat without actually drowning. After the departure of the Romans in the 5th century their baths fell out of use, not being part of the culture of succeeding waves of invaders. During the Middle Ages the idea of swimming as a useful military skill and signifier of manly prowess persisted, although fewer and fewer actually pursued the activity.

There had not been a great deal of progress on the hygiene front by the late 16th century, even though the Church considered that 'cleanliness was next to godliness' and it was said, apocryphally, that Queen Elizabeth I took a bath once a month whether she needed it or not. There was, however, a revival of interest in the classics and the exploits of the Romans. Young men were once again encouraged to swim, not just for military purposes but for their own fitness and health. It was at this time that the first known book about swimming appeared. In 1587 Sir Everard Digby published *De Arte Natandi*, illustrated with helpful woodcuts, as a swimming manual for youths of good birth (Latin scholars at least) to help them avoid danger while cooling off in rivers in the summer. The limited readership increased slightly in 1595 when an English edition was produced.

Some of the normal populace enjoyed taking a dip in ponds, lakes and rivers, not always in great safety. Londoners swam in the polluted waters of the Rivers Thames and Fleet. In Cambridge the university banned 'swimming in the River Cam or any other river, pond or water within the county' because of the number of accidents and drownings.

This led to a few institutions and wealthy individuals, mostly in southern England, establishing private pools for the use of 'gentlemen' who could afford to pay for the privilege. The vast majority of the population remained unable to swim, nor had any idea that they wanted to; up until the 18th century the British coast was associated only with ports and fishing.

All this was to change. The upper classes had been used to easing their various aches and pains by bathing in and drinking from mineral springs found in inland spas, such as Bath and Harrogate, and at the coastal town of Scarborough where the spring issued from the base of a cliff. In the mid-17th century, local doctor Robert Wittie, having analysed the water, began to wonder if the use of the even more mineral-rich sea water could have even greater benefits. (His book, *Scarborough Spaw*, was published in 1660.) Actual immersion in the sea was also promoted by those who championed the cure-all properties of cold water, summarised in Sir John Floyer's 1715 treatise *The History of Cold Bathing*. Thus Scarborough had all the requirements for the perfect restorative regimen – a few pints of spring or sea water, five minutes up to the neck in the bracing North Sea followed by a bout of vigorous exercise on the broad sandy beach.

The ideas spread and in 1750 another doctor, Richard Russell, published his *Dissertation on the Use of Sea Water in the Diseases of the Glands*. Queues of wealthy and fashionable hypochondriacs built up at his surgery in Brighton; the new craze took off. Following a similar ritual to that of a normal spa session, patients were advised to immerse themselves in the sea, the colder the better – winter being the preferred season for the first seaside visits. The brief dip was followed by a reviving glass of sea water, often mixed with milk and honey. This prescription was unlikely to remain popular for long. Drinking sea water was neither pleasant, safe nor health-enhancing. More delicate souls preferred to bathe when there was less chance of freezing on emerging from the sea or of suffering a heart attack from the sudden shock of the cold. Thus the season for bathing shifted and lengthened. As the benefits of bathing and breathing the sea air reached a wider audience, more and more people were attracted to the coast, leading to the establishment of a new type of settlement – the seaside resort.

This soon became the preferred destination for the aristocracy who were mortified to discover that well-off tradespeople and members of the burgeoning middle classes were now able to afford time in traditional haunts like Bath. The fashionable new locations were coastal towns, mainly in the south of England, although Scarborough in Yorkshire also flourished, having a justifiable claim to be Britain's first holiday resort. Even royalty got in on the act; George III popularised Weymouth while the Prince Regent (later George IV) championed Brighton. As bathing took only a small proportion of the day and simple promenading could eventually become wearisome, further diversions were sought. Places to provide refreshment, to listen to music and quiet garden areas in which to sit and relax began to appear along with shops, theatres and sporting venues, laying the foundations for the seaside resort as we know it.

At this time such places were the exclusive preserve of the wealthy. Only they had the time and the means to undertake a journey to the coast and establish themselves there in reasonable comfort. Relatives, however distant, with a property within sight of the sea, would find that they were enjoying increased popularity. The Prince Regent indulged himself and his entourage with quite spectacular accommodation in his exotic Royal Pavilion for their sojourns by the sea in Brighton. This was a far cry from the lot of the working classes, often packed together in the expanding industrial towns of the north, with barely an hour to spare after Sunday worship and for whom a day at the seaside must have seemed an impossible dream.

Morecambe had not been part of this first wave of seaside development. In fact it did not exist as such; the small fishing village of Poulton-le-Sands sat beside its equally small neighbours, Bare, Torrisholme and Heysham on the south-east coast of Morecambe Bay, a few miles from the more important town of Lancaster. However, in the early 19th century Poulton had started to attract visitors; coach services brought people from Lancaster while considerable numbers came from a little further afield. Their purpose was not to swim but to take advantage of the 'physic in the sea', the belief that seawater contained beneficial medical ingredients which would cure or alleviate all manner of ailments. This was a very different clientele from the wealthy patrons who frequented the more genteel resorts in the south of England. The visitors who descended on Poulton and neighbouring coastal settlements in their thousands, by cart or on foot, were working-class men and women from the mills and factories of inland Lancashire. This influx tended to occur at one particular time of the year, coinciding with the high (spring) tides in August and September when the medicinal properties of the seawater were supposedly at their strongest.

On a tour of Britain in 1814 the writer Richard Ayton arrived in Poulton in August on the first day of a spring tide and found it overwhelmed with visitors and the beach "darkened with thick clusters of people, full of motion, and continuously splashing in and out of the water". He struggled to find accommodation for the night, most inns and cottages being full to bursting. Their owners, aware there was money to be made from this annual invasion, crammed as many beds as possible into each room and several people into each bed.

The visitors, Ayton discovered, "rest here only three or four days and in each of these undergo a course of seasoning [in which] each morning they take a draught of seawater, a quart and sometimes two, which is followed, under the notion of fortifying the stomach, by an equal quantity of gin and beer". Having swallowed this mixture (and survived) an individual is then "properly prepared for the bath [sea] in which he continues to paddle, either in or out of his clothes, for the remainder of the day".

While imbibing large quantities of seawater probably did more harm than good, other parts of the regimen (breathing sea air and bathing in the sea) were seen as having beneficial effects on health and well-being. Promenading and paddling became the vogue and a more discerning class of visitor began to arrive in Poulton. By 1840 a number of marine villas had been built facing the sea, advertised as being suitable for 'families of the most respectable rank'.

The village was starting to grow, gradually outstripping its neighbours. However, the catalyst that really sparked the surge in population, which Poulton and many similar settlements experienced, was the railway. Once the pulling power of the steam locomotive had been successfully demonstrated, railway mania swept the country. Companies sprang up, racing to build lines to connect the inland industrial towns with the ports. Not only could trains transport large amounts of freight, they could also transport people in great numbers. Morecambe's turn was about to come.

Its larger neighbour, Lancaster, was struggling in its role as a port; ships were getting bigger and the River Lune was becoming shallower as the estuary silted up. This was further complicated when the viaduct carrying the west coast railway to Scotland was built over the Lune, hampering still more the flow of river traffic. A decision was made to create a new port, to be named Morecambe Bay Harbour, close to the village of Poulton and linked directly to Lancaster. The first idea, to join the two by ship canal, was shelved because of cost and was replaced by a railway. In 1848 the 'Little North Western' line connected Lancaster to the new harbour. By 1850 the line had been extended to West Yorkshire. It brought businessmen and tradesmen to the port, industrial goods for export – and visitors eager for a sight of the sea.

The summer of 1850 witnessed a huge influx of day-trippers arriving by train – outings from mills and Sunday Schools from towns like Bradford and Leeds. Morecambe Bay Harbour, being rather a mouthful to say and rather long to print on signs and tickets, soon contracted to Morecambe and replaced Poulton as the name for the whole settlement, village and harbour combined. Seaside activities rapidly started to overtake those of the port as the mainstay of Morecambe's existence. By the 1880s the harbour was losing trade to other, bigger ports and was experiencing its own problems with silting and loss of water depth. The business of pleasure, however, was booming.

While the first visitors came to bathe in the sea as a form of hydrotherapy, it was not long before people realised it could actually be enjoyable in its own right. As soon as fun was introduced there were immediate concerns that 'sea bathing could incite lasciviousness and immorality'. A strict etiquette developed, backed up by numerous regulations about how, where and when it was permitted to enter the water. The sexes had, of course, to be kept separate – in some resorts leading to the use of completely different beaches. To prevent a glimpse of even so much as an ankle, all changing and entering the sea had to be via a bathing machine or van, as it was known in Morecambe.

In appearance the vans resembled simple garden sheds on wheels with the means for horses to be able to pull them in and out of the water. The bather would enter via a short flight of wooden steps, get undressed in the dim light penetrating from a small high window and then put on a bathing dress. In the early days this meant basically nothing at all for men (the more skin exposed to the sea water, the greater the health benefits) whereas for women, capes, bonnets, stockings and skirts weighted down at the hem (to avoid exposure of the lower limbs) were the norm. There were gradual moves towards equality of dress with men wearing more, progressing through a long-johns type of garment to a shapeless all-in-one, buttoned at the neck and reaching to below the knees. Women, meanwhile, reversed the process, shedding layers, going through a phase of nightgown-like apparel to eventually reach a similar state to the men and often topped off with a mob-cap to protect their hair.

In this scene of around 1910 ranks of bathing machines or vans are lined up on the beach near the Stone Jetty, the cold and blustery conditions precluding their use. In line with the idea of sea bathing as a form of medication, the vans' sides are emblazoned with advertisements for another 'cure-all', Beecham's Pills. In fine weather horses would pull the vans to the water's edge allowing bathers to reach the deeper channel near the end of the jetty and then return them safely after their brief immersion. Many of the vans on this section of the beach were owned by William Forbes Anderson who also ran goat-cart and donkey rides on the foreshore.

Once attired, the bather and van were pulled down the beach to the sea, accompanied by an attendant or 'dipper'. When a sufficient depth of water had been reached the bather would leave the van, descend the steps and immerse themselves in the sea, helped by the attendant if they appeared reluctant. The main objective was not to swim, as few people could, but to take advantage of the restorative powers of the seawater.

Immersion would be brief as vans were usually hired for the half hour only. Victorian ladies were advised: 'Two hours after breakfast, get undressed quickly … take a quick succession of dips up to the chin and get out into the machine after five minutes.' If their teeth chattered or they appeared blue round the mouth, brandy was recommended while dressing. The thick, woolly nature of the costumes worn meant they absorbed a considerable weight of water making any movement in the sea almost impossible and necessitating the assistance of the attendant to return to the van. Bather and van would then be pulled back above the water line for the drying and dressing process to be completed.

By the end of the 19th century many visitors, especially those who had travelled and experienced the freer regimes on the continent, began to resent the strict rules laid down in Britain. Fearing the loss of their wealthier clients some resorts began to relax their by-laws, replacing bathing machines with changing huts or tents and allowing

Bathing machines had generally fallen out of use by the 1920s but some clung on in Morecambe for a further decade when the last few either found a new use as a changing room in a local school, a shed on an allotment or part of a ceremonial bonfire.

people to bathe from the shore. Morecambe, catering more for the working class visitor, did not permit this until 1923 but it was still not acceptable to change on the beach. To avoid the cost of hiring a hut or tent, people would change at home or in their lodgings and proceed to the beach enveloped in a dressing gown or coat, a practice which became known as 'mackintosh bathing'. It was well into the 1930s before the idea of paying for and, therefore, restricting access to the sea died out. By then holiday resorts had found many other ingenious methods of parting visitors from their money.

For some, sea bathing appeared both difficult and dangerous. In the second half of the 19th century the needs of many people for baths for cleanliness and health, coupled with the desire of others for safe places to swim, led a number of councils and enlightened individuals to provide pools or baths for the public. In 1867 a Mr Dickinson opened Morecambe's first public baths in Green Street which took in sea water via pipes under the promenade, later supplemented by fresh water and hot sulphur baths. The lower classes were allowed to use these facilities on Saturday afternoons. In Lancaster, Samuel Gregson, working on a rather more ambitious scale, built and donated Cable Street baths to the town in 1863. They were large enough to provide exercise and enjoyment for the working man as well as hygiene. Women were not so fortunate; in 1870 they were still pleading with the authorities to be allowed the use of the baths for half a day a week.

Extending the use of these and other amenities to all was of little use without the time for all to enjoy them. The Bank Holidays Act of 1871, allowing certain guaranteed days off work, went a little way to address this. (For most people, a longer vacation was not a possibility until another Act of Parliament, in 1938, introduced holidays with pay.)

On summer Bank Holidays thousands flocked to Morecambe for the day. The Midland Railway ran special advertising campaigns in West Yorkshire, with cheap excursion tickets. It was as if the entire population of Leeds and Bradford had descended on the streets of Morecambe.

As a response to the demands of visitors of all types, the town experienced a great wave of building. It acquired shops, hotels, restaurants, dance halls, theatres, piers, Summer Gardens and, in 1878, the crowning glory of the Winter Gardens. In a *Topography and Directory of Lancaster and Ten Miles Around,* the writer describes 'Poulton-le-Sands, now better known as Morecambe' as a 'clean, healthy and popular watering place', commenting on its rapid growth over the last few years. Of special note was 'the crescent opposite the bay ... a fine range of buildings ... first class Hotels, several Bazaars and the Morecambe Baths, Palace and Aquarium, a place much resorted to for recreation and amusement and in which are two public baths for gentlemen and one for ladies' (see page 12). Thus the Winter Gardens provided Morecambe with its first pools large enough for swimming. Sadly, they had a very brief existence, giving way, in 1896, to even more popular forms of entertainment – wining, dining and the music hall. The baths' presence is remembered in the names of Bath Street and the Bath Hotel situated behind the present Winter Gardens building.

Interest in the actual activity of swimming was growing. Men who could swim often sought to profit from this, awarding themselves the honorary title of 'Professor', tutoring their wealthy gentlemen clients in the arts of 'natation'. They also promoted the sport as a form of entertainment with diving displays and daring underwater stunts as part of general variety shows.

A sign which used to hang outside the Bath Hotel during the 20th century harking back to the 19th century baths at the Winter Gardens.

Serious swimming was given a considerable boost by the news of Captain Matthew Webb's exploits in the English Channel. Having trained and worked as a mariner, Webb turned to professional swimming in his late twenties and on 25th August 1875 he became the first person to successfully swim from Dover to Calais. Soon other intrepid young men (and women) were practising this and other feats of endurance – long distance swimmers became the superstars of the day.

In order to further the activity, groups of like-minded individuals came together to form swimming clubs, usually where there were indoor pools. Morecambe's first such associations, the Victoria Swimming Club of Bare and the West End Swimming Club,

MORECAMBE
BATHS, PALACE, AND AQUARIUM.
PURE FILTERED
SEA WATER BATHS.

GENTLEMEN'S BATHS.

FIRST CLASS TEPID PLUNGE,

60 feet by 28 feet. Temperature is maintained many degrees higher than temperature of Sea Water. Dressing Boxes well Furnished and Warmed. Fresh Cold Water Shower attached.

SECOND CLASS TEPID PLUNGE,

73 feet by 28 feet. Dressing Boxes Warmed. A Splendid Bath. Fresh Cold Shower attached.

FIRST CLASS PRIVATE,

Any Temperature. SALT, COLD, FRESH SHOWER, VAPOUR and HOT-AIR BATHS &c. Dressing Boxes well Furnished. Comfortable and scrupulously clean. Sheet, Towels, and Attendant.

SECOND CLASS PRIVATE, Light, Roomy, well Ventilated and Warmed.

LADIES' BATHS.

FIRST CLASS TEPID PLUNGE, 60 feet by 28 feet.

Pronounced by all to be a beautiful Bath Room, and comfortable Dressing Boxes. Bathing Costumes provided. Dressing Boxes amply furnished and Warmed. Fresh Cold Shower attached.

FIRST CLASS PRIVATE,

Any temperature. Salt, Cold, Fresh, and Shower. Dressing Rooms scrupulously Clean, Lighted, well Ventilated, Warmed, and Furnished. VAPOUR and HOT AIR BATHS, etc. Sheet, Towels, and Attendant.

SECOND CLASS PRIVATE, Light, Roomy, well Ventilated and Warmed

Open Week Days, 7am to 8-30pm; Mondays & Thursdays, 6-30am to 8-30pm; Sundays, 7am to 10am

PRICES =

Resident Season Tickets to all Baths (not Transferable) .. .. £2 2s. per Annum
Resident Season Tickets to Large and Plunge (not Transferable) .. .. £1 1s. per Annum

First Class Tepid Plunge, Single Ticket 1s
    For Families   Twelve Tickets .. .. 10s   Two Towels, Costumes or Drawers provided
                         Twenty-five Tickets 20s

Second Class Plunge, Single Ticket 6d
    For Families   Twelve Tickets .. .. 5s   One Towel, Costumes or Drawers provided
                         Twenty-five Tickets 10s

First Class Private, Single Ticket .. .. 2s   Medicated Bath, Single Ticket 2s 6d
    For Families   Twelve Tickets .. .. 20s   For Families   Twelve Tickets 23s
                         Twenty-five Tickets .. .. 40s   Twenty-five Tickets .. 50s

Second Class Private Baths, Single Ticket 1s; Twelve Tickets 10s; Twenty-five Tickets 20s

Special Arrangements made with Schools

Mr. J. L. SHORROCK, General Manager

both founded in 1905, were restricted to using the waters of Morecambe Bay. Despite this, when both held their first Annual General Meetings in February 1906, they were able to declare themselves satisfied with their success in encouraging local people to swim.

It was reported that the Victoria Swimming Club's membership of one hundred and fifty (including ladies) had enjoyed weather conducive to swimming throughout the season but were disappointed that inclement conditions on the day in August, fixed for their inaugural gala, had forced its postponement. Committee members were considering putting forward a proposal to Morecambe Corporation which would prevent this happening in the future. They wanted a swimming pool.

This would be safer than bathing in the sea, would offer calm rather than rough water and would allow bathing at any hour irrespective of the state of the tide. They quoted the words of a respected visitor from the previous season, Mr A. Laird, the 'Father of Scotch Swimming', who had said that the club "could never expect to attain great success in teaching the art of swimming to the young unless a bathing pool or bath was provided, as tuition in the open sea, where the waves broke upon them during instruction in the art, frightened the learners and caused them to lose confidence". The committee hoped to persuade the Corporation of the benefits to the town by pointing out the popularity of galas, water polo matches and other water sports which could be held at the pool and attract paying spectators. Morecambe could be advertised as a 'Health and Pleasure Resort'.

In March 1906 councillors gave the go-ahead to the project, although not without the usual misgivings about expense. There was also the vexed question of whether there would be strict enough control and that the 'no Sunday bathing' rule would be adhered to. Speaking in favour of the plan, Alderman Carleton stated: "It was very wrong that the

Bare pool, built at the request of the Victoria Swimming Club, opened in August 1906. The crowds of spectators lining the ramp clearly outnumber the children paddling round the edge or the brave souls actually swimming.

In its heyday Bare pool was a popular rendezvous for serious swimmers and sea-bathers, especially, as here, when the tide was out.

majority of Morecambe fishermen, who went out with the boats, could not swim. Then there was the additional advantage in that the elementary scholars would be taught to swim and ultimately save life."

A simple wall was built to enclose a sea water pool with a ramp on one side leading from the changing facilities to the water. True to form for such enterprises it was not completed in time for its publicised opening day in mid-July when Scottish international swimmers, visiting Lancaster, had been invited to perform 'some of their clever natatory evolutions'. Eventually, on 15th August 1906, the Victoria Swimming Club was given permission to take possession of the completed pool. Despite worries that the late start to the season would lead to financial hardship, the pool prospered, continuing to provide a worthwhile amenity for many years before being taken over by Morecambe Corporation when the club no longer wished to run it.

Initially, the large number of bathers and onlookers caused worries about organisation. It was proposed that 'one capable official should be in sole charge and he should be dressed in uniform or at least wear a cap with the words *Victoria Swimming Club* emblazoned upon it, if only to stamp him with a little authority'. Another concern was the dressing accommodation, a van sited at the top of the slipway, divided into eight cubicles. This was too few in number and the cubicles were too big for one person but the thought of being occupied by more than one was extremely distasteful. The problem was solved when the van was swept away in a storm and replaced by a more substantial structure, later supplemented by additional bathing huts and tents.

For the genteel population of Bare, propriety remained a pressing concern even into the 1930s as an article in the *Visitor* newspaper of June 1936 highlighted. 'The ladies' dressing tent is only to be got at by going through the men's. For a moderate sum male bathers may lounge about in their alley-way and feast their eyes on female beauty passing in and out. Those who object to paying this trifling sum may stand around outside and get a very good, but more distant view, as the ladies make their fifty yards pilgrimage to and from the water.' The shock to the system of what was shortly to transpire in central Morecambe must have been tremendous.

Back in 1907, the desire for pools having been satisfied both in Bare and in the West End at Sandylands, the local swimmers set their sights further afield. If the bay could be crossed on foot or by horse and cart when the tide was out, could it be swum across when the tide was in? A group consisting of the Bare, West End and Lancaster Swimming Clubs decided to try and the Morecambe Cross Bay Swimming Association was born. Having made one or two failed attempts themselves, the local swimmers decided to consult an expert, convinced that a good professional could do it and that their dream of an annual Cross Bay Championship might be realised.

On 13th July 1907 'Professor' William Stearne, a professional swimmer from Manchester, became the first to swim successfully from Grange-over-Sands to Morecambe. Stearne was a strong, six foot, fifteen stone individual who, at the age of forty-one, was in training for an attempt at the English Channel. He made serious preparations for his swim; before setting off from Grange he reportedly ate a hearty meal of bread, soup, steak, potatoes, even more bread and, as an afterthought, two helpings of salmon. While swimming, he also consumed about a dozen eggs, two pints of milk, two pints of beef tea and pieces of chicken, all supplied to him from his escort boat. Partway across he found his costume had become too heavy and irksome for comfortable swimming and so discarded it, which meant that when he finally reached Morecambe, three and three quarter hours after leaving Grange, he was forced to exit the water backwards to avoid alarming the enthusiastic crowd which had gathered to greet him. A collection had been taken on Grange promenade from the spectators seeing him off and another was made when he stepped ashore at Morecambe; seventy-five percent went to the Professor and twenty-five percent to enable the Cross Bay Swimming Association to start its championship.

The first season, though short, created a fair amount of interest and the dinner and prize-giving on 30th October 1907 at the Clarendon Hotel was well attended. The

This cartoon, reproduced on a postcard sent in 1910, illustrates two popular leisure pursuits of the time. Improvements in photographic processes had led to the development of hand-held cameras such as George Eastman's 1900 Kodak Brownie priced at five shillings. While not in the reach of everyone's pocket, it was both cheap and simple enough for widespread use. The growing trend for mixed bathing meant a certain loss of privacy for female bathers while their increasingly revealing costumes provided an irresistible subject for amateur and professional photographers alike.

In August 1912, it was reported that, at Bare pool, 'a young lady, bolder than many, took part in knocking a water polo ball about among the men but the greatest feature was the two gentlemen with a cinematograph who got some really interesting pictures which were shown at the Winter Gardens'.

Even after the opening of the Super Swimming Stadium, Bare pool was a safe haven for bathers, particularly children, and somewhere to catch the sun. As beach materials gradually built up on the bottom of the pool, the depth of water decreased making it more suitable for paddling and model boats in its later days.

mayor, Councillor Samuel Wright, presented the first champion, Mr Brierley Law of Chadderton, with a silver shield donated by Lord Ashton and a diamond ring. The runner-up, Mr McMahon of Preston, received a gold watch and the oarsman of the winner's pilot boat, Mr John Woodhouse, took home an oak clock. The prizes were paid for by subscription, the most generous donor being Lord Ashton and the remainder being made up by councillors and the general public.

There was a general air of congratulation. The swimmers were commended for their times (3 hours and 5 minutes for Law) and William Stearne vowed he would return the following year to better it, perhaps inspired by Law's approach of not stopping for afternoon tea half way across. The course was declared to be a good length, not overlong like the English Channel, and Lord Ashton expressed confidence that the Cross Bay Championship would become a permanent fixture, bringing much acclaim and a great many visitors to Morecambe. Better and more far-reaching advertising was recommended and there was a fervent hope that now they had seen that the swim was possible, more local fishermen would volunteer their services as escorts.

The fishermen were crucial to the success of the swim; they had the knowledge of tides, currents and the layout of the channels and sand banks of the bay. They would also be the best judges of the course to take, which could vary in position and distance from year to year due to changing conditions, and they made ideal pilots for the support boats.

The procedure as explained by Charlie Overett (an ex-fisherman who piloted for swims in the early 1960s) was that an experienced fisherman would be the main pilot, taking his trawler from Morecambe to Grange with a flotilla of small rowing boats in tow. These contained the competitors and their personal pilots, often no more than teenagers but sufficiently experienced and strong enough to row from Grange back to Morecambe. Everyone would gather on Grange promenade and at the right point of the tide the swimmers would wade into the sea (the idea of a dive-in from a jetty having long since been abandoned). At a signal from a timekeeper they would then begin to swim.

A fine summer's day in the early 1950s draws an interested crowd of spectators to the promenade at Grange-over-Sands to witness the start of the Cross Bay Swim. The competitors wade out and the pilots ready their small craft to await the signal from the timekeeper to set off.

It was the job of the rowers to stay with their swimmers, keeping them more or less on the route planned by the chief pilot. Using their knowledge of local landmarks and buoys they tried to allow the swimmers to benefit from tides and currents while at the same time preventing them from becoming stranded on sandbanks or being swept past the prescribed landing site. They were also responsible for the safety of the swimmers, rescuing any overcome by cold or exhaustion. The course was completed when a swimmer reached a point between the Stone Jetty and the West End Pier and could stand to wade ashore, raising their arms above their head to show that they had finished. There were usually several swims a season, the number depending on the weather. At first the person with the fastest time from any of these was declared the champion but later the September event became a final for the men who had competed well in the previous crossings. (Women continued with the best overall time.)

The competition attracted long distance swimmers from far and wide, many in training for attempts on the English Channel; several said it was just as challenging and even colder. The Chadderton Swimming Club which had provided the first winner, Brierly Law, also produced one of the most noted competitors, Harry Taylor, who won the championship on sixteen occasions, setting a record time of just over two hours in 1914. This must have been a good year with fine weather and a shorter, more direct course as the ladies' record was also set that year. Taylor was a freestyle swimmer who represented Great Britain at Olympic Games from 1906 to 1920 and was, incidentally, for a while, manager of Bare bathing pool.

Often a swimmer would form a good working relationship with a particular pilot. Charlie Overett has fond memories of two competitors in particular. One was a well-built young lady from Bradford named Dorothy Perkins who had swum the English Channel aged nineteen and competed in the Cross Bay Championships in her twenties. The other was Commander Charles Gerald Forsberg, a renowned long-distance swimmer,

Rough weather frequently caused the postponement of the Cross Bay Swim. On this occasion, in order not to disappoint the large crowd which had already gathered at Grange-over-Sands to see the competitors off, two former champions, Miss K. Hodgson and Miss F. Blackburn, volunteered to give the spectators a demonstration. Here they can be seen swimming hard in choppy water along the coast accompanied by a pilot boat.

Shown here, in the centre foreground, with their pilots and an admiring crowd are Dorothy Simpson of Morecambe and Kathleen Hodgson of Grange-over-Sands, joint lady champions of the 1937 Cross Bay Swim, who won their race in a dead heat of 4 hours and 50 minutes.

Charles Daly of Manchester is given a helping hand ashore by the mayor, Councillor Michael Benson, on 7th August 1937. He was one of only two competitors who completed the Cross Bay Swim that day, finishing in 3 hours 45 minutes, having swum 'with the precision of a machine all the way'. On reaching Morecambe 'he swam below cheering crowds on the Pier and along to the landing stage near the baths where he finished amidst loud cheers from thousands of people who were assembled on the steps of the sea wall'. After his warm welcome he made the unfortunate discovery that the case containing his dry clothes was not in the pilot boat but had been left behind at Grange Baths. Undaunted, he changed into a dry bathing costume and dressing gown and walked to the Crown Hotel where he sat and read for three hours while a friend brought back his clothes by train from Grange. Daly took part in the Cross Bay Swim 29 times, winning the championship on three occasions.

The Nottingham based long-distance swimmer Tom Blower, known as the 'Human Torpedo', chats to Mayor Benson before a crowd of hero-worshipping youngsters in August 1937. He had recently swum the English Channel in a record time and in September would become Cross Bay Champion for the third year in succession. He said later of that swim: "It was terrible. It was blowing a gale out in the Bay. I've never swum in water half as rough. It's the worst swim I've ever experienced, including the Channel."

This memorial on the promenade in Morecambe's West End was presented by the British Long Distance Swimming Association to honour Commander 'Gerry' Forsberg. Born in Canada, Forsberg was involved with the sea all his life, serving with distinction in the Royal Navy during the Second World War. His love of marathon swimming led him across Loch Lomond and Loch Ness, Lough Neagh, Windermere and the English Channel (he held the record in 1957) as well as Morecambe Bay which he loved so much. He was still entering outdoor competitions in his eighties and going for a daily dip in Sandylands pool.

who also included the English Channel among his conquests and who competed twenty-nine times in Morecambe Bay. In 1960 he became the first champion of the two-way swim from Morecambe to Grange and back (in 6 hours and 23 minutes) while Dorothy Perkins took the ladies' title.

From the late 1960s Morecambe's fishing fleet shrank markedly and it became increasingly difficult to find sufficient pilots to support the swimmers. Conditions in the bay also changed so that it became more dangerous to attempt the crossing and alternative swims within the bay were tried. The British Long Distance Swimming Association took over the organisation but the popularity of the Cross Bay event steadily declined and it has not been a feature since the 1990s.

During the first two decades of the 20th century Morecambe had been adding to its amenities to attract the modern visitor, so it was rather against the trend when, in 1926, there was a move to return to the idea of a health spa. On the promenade, almost opposite the Winter Gardens, there appeared a glass and fretwork structure known as the Kursaal. Here people were invited to drink mineral water at 3d a glass, efficacious in the treatment of liver complaints, rheumatism, gout, dyspepsia, constipation and, if nothing else, as a general pick-me-up. As Morecambe had no mineral springs of its own the precious water was transported daily, by train, from the Holy Well at Humphrey Head on the other side of the bay.

The venture was not a resounding success and the building soon fell out of use and was eventually demolished in 1950. It was not what the typical tourist expected from Morecambe. Many were coming from the industrial towns of West Yorkshire in search of fresh air and fun, not the gentility of a spa. Morecambe may well have been seen as Bradford-by-the-Sea but it was never going to be Harrogate-sur-la-Mer. If it was to be the up-and-coming resort of the Corporation's dreams, it had to provide what people wanted. It had places to stay, places to eat, glorious views and amusements galore; now what it needed, what any self-respecting modern seaside resort must have and what its close neighbours and rivals were getting, was a big, beautiful, state of the art swimming pool.

With or without a swimming pool, people still wanted to go for a dip in the sea. Here Morecambe's promenade and beach are thronged with day-trippers and holidaymakers enjoying the sunshine. Many of those in the sea are dressed for the occasion, albeit in the saggy woollen costumes of the time, but others, unable to resist the opportunity for a paddle, have the typical holiday attire of best suit with trouser legs rolled up or skirt firmly tucked into underwear.

THE BEST LAID PLANS ...

TWO

The growing popularity of swimming as a leisure pursuit and for improving health and fitness was encouraging many seaside resorts to invest in the construction of new open-air pools, or lidos. In the north-west of England one of the first places to do so was Blackpool. Never a town to do anything in half measures, its new swimming pool was huge in scale, measuring 376 feet (116 metres) by 172 feet (53 metres) and able to accommodate 3,000 spectators. Claimed, with some justification, by Blackpool Corporation to be 'the finest pool in the whole world' when it opened in 1923, it cost a staggering £80,000 and attracted over half a million swimmers and spectators in its first full season. When compared with later examples, its classically influenced architecture, though in vogue at the time, seemed rooted in the past – more Beaux Arts than Bauhaus. Nevertheless, its remarkable success had not gone unnoticed twenty miles further north along the Lancashire coast.

By the late 1920s Morecambe had developed into a thriving holiday resort with tens of thousands of visitors swelling the population during the summer months. While conceding that Blackpool was more popular in terms of numbers, Morecambe always considered itself to be somewhat more refined and upmarket than its brash neighbour, appealing to a more discerning class of holidaymaker. Among its attractions the town could boast two piers, four theatres, four concert party pavilions, four cinemas, an amusement park, a golf course, two large parks with tennis courts and bowling greens – but no swimming pool, a facility regarded as essential to a modern seaside resort as a pier was in Victorian times. This was an omission Morecambe Corporation was keen to rectify, especially as the Government was offering loans to local authorities to carry out works commissioned in the public interest to generate employment in a time of great economic depression.

Once the decision was taken to go ahead, Morecambe's councillors were then faced with confronting the logistics of the project. Where should the swimming pool be located? Who should design and build it? How much would it cost? Discussions occupied the early weeks of 1927 and by the end of March it had been agreed that the best site for the new pool would be on the foreshore opposite the town's Winter Gardens. However, as a consensus could not be reached regarding its design and construction, councillors voted to hold a competition the details of which were outlined in the *Visitor* of March 30th. 'With reference to the proposed Bathing Pool which is to be constructed opposite the Winter Gardens on some future date yet unknown, the Town Clerk reported to the Advertising and Entertainment Committee that the President of RIBA [Royal Institute of British Architects] had, at the request of the Committee, appointed Mr Gilbert Fraser, FRIBA, of Wellington Buildings, Strand, Liverpool, to act as Assessor in the competition for the best designs for the Pool.'

Gilbert Fraser's remit was to select six leading architects to take part in the competition, their entries to be delivered by 30th June 1927. After due consideration the first prize of £100 was awarded to the London based architects K.M.B. Cross & A.W. Sutton. The Lancaster firm of T.H. Mawson & Sons came second and received £50, while Easton & Robertson of London collected £25 for third place. Holding a competition for the design of a swimming pool was an exception to the norm as most open-air pools/lidos, were designed not by practising architects but by borough engineers or surveyors. Kenneth

Watercolour sketch of the proposed swimming pool for Morecambe by Cyril A. Farey 1927.

Cross, one of the winning architects and later President of RIBA, was a vociferous critic of the way local authorities commissioned such pools, considering that in many cases it resulted in buildings of little or no architectural merit.

This certainly could not be said of Cross & Sutton's plans for Morecambe's new swimming stadium. Set in a large basin and separated from the bay only by a new sea wall and promenade, the striking white building was pleasing to the eye from all sides. Essentially rectangular in plan with curved ends, its overall shape was a nod to modernity although it still included the towers, domes and columns beloved by an earlier generation of architects. The broad walkways and roof-top terraces were an encouragement to visitors to stroll in the invigorating sea air or bathe in the now-fashionable sunshine even if they could not be persuaded to actually take a dip in the pool. In its landscaped surroundings other activities would be catered for such as lawn tennis, a sport increasingly popular with both sexes.

The whole project, including the swimming pool and its environs, Turkish and medicated baths and the construction of a new promenade, was estimated to cost a total of £63,388. Such was their enthusiasm that Morecambe's councillors approved the proposals without a dissenting voice. The *Visitor* was equally positive. 'The scheme is an elaborate one, and when finished will furnish Morecambe with one of the most up-to-date baths in the country. It is hoped to start the work of the first part of the scheme at the end of this year.' Never was such optimism so misplaced. Nearly another decade would pass before the first swimmers would be able to take the plunge into the town's new pool.

KENNETH CROSS (Architect)

Kenneth Cross, with his partner Cecil Sutton, won the competition to design Morecambe's new swimming pool in 1927. Born into a well-to-do family in 1890, he was the son of architect Alfred Cross and studied history and architecture at Cambridge University before setting up in private practice in 1919. Three years later he became a partner in his father's firm and acted as architect for a number of local authorities including Westminster, Newcastle and Bournemouth councils. Like his father he earned a reputation as a specialist in the design and construction of swimming baths and together they published a book on the subject entitled *Modern Public Baths and Wash-Houses* in 1930. Having been elected a fellow of RIBA in 1932 he worked tirelessly for the Institute for many years, eventually becoming its president in 1956. As well as being responsible for the Super Swimming Stadium, Cross & Sutton also designed the façade for Morecambe's new Town Hall which opened in 1932. Kenneth Cross died in 1968.

Although a site for the baths had been identified, the size and scale of Cross & Sutton's winning design meant that the amount of land available would be insufficient for the proposed building. In addition, the location was susceptible to flooding on high tides, a drawback more than one letter to the *Visitor* was not slow to point out. Morecambe Corporation's problem was that most of the land on the seaward side of Marine Road was owned by the London, Midland and Scottish Railway. This included the Old Harbour which the railway company had leased as a shipbreaking yard to the Sheffield firm of T.W. Ward Ltd since 1905. Over the ensuing years the noise and pollution produced by the demolition process had generated numerous complaints from local people who considered Ward's presence to be a blight on the seafront and wholly inappropriate for a holiday resort or, as the *Visitor* succinctly put it, 'a blot on Morecambe's fair face'. While many councillors were sympathetic towards these concerns they were willing to tolerate the disturbance as the business provided much needed employment for some 200 workers and had, ironically, also become a popular tourist attraction. Over the years thousands of people paid to look round the condemned vessels, the most famous of which was the White Star liner *Majestic*, sister ship to the ill-fated *Titanic*.

However, by the late 1920s attitudes towards the shipbreaking firm were changing and Morecambe Corporation had begun to investigate the possibility of integrating the Old Harbour site into a scheme for improving the seafront and creating a more attractive environment. For its part the LMS was willing to sell the land if a satisfactory price could be negotiated. Before it could purchase the site the Corporation would need to gain authorisation from the Government to borrow the required money and this necessitated the passing of a Parliamentary Bill. Unsurprisingly, the proposal was vehemently opposed by Ward's who embarked on a spate of pamphleteering, urging opposition to the Bill. Firmly siding with the Corporation, the *Visitor* countered with headlines such as 'Away with the Blot' and 'Remove the Eyesore' and pictures showing the improvement which would result if the old shipbreaking yard was replaced by modern attractions. At a packed and heated pubic meeting in May 1928 to decide if the Bill should proceed, the combined forces of Ward's management and employees failed to convince enough people of their case and the Bill went forward, eventually being passed three months later.

Even if Ward's had been successful its continued occupation of the site would have been relatively short-lived as the LMS had decided to replace its ageing and run-down Midland Hotel next to the Old Harbour with a brand new building. Worried about the negative effects the activities of the adjacent shipbreaking yard might have on the proposed hotel and its guests, the railway company gave notice to Ward's that its lease would be coming to an end. A price of £34,000 for the Old Harbour site was agreed but the LMS would only sell when it was satisfied that the Corporation was in a position to proceed with the construction of a promenade and other seafront improvements. This would take a further three years.

During this time the plans for the new Midland Hotel underwent revision resulting in less space being required for the building. The surplus land was offered to Morecambe Corporation for £23,000 with the proviso that the latter 'may only erect pleasure gardens or other buildings which will not interfere with the amenities of the hotel'. This was accepted and in December 1931 a contract for the sale of the Old Harbour site

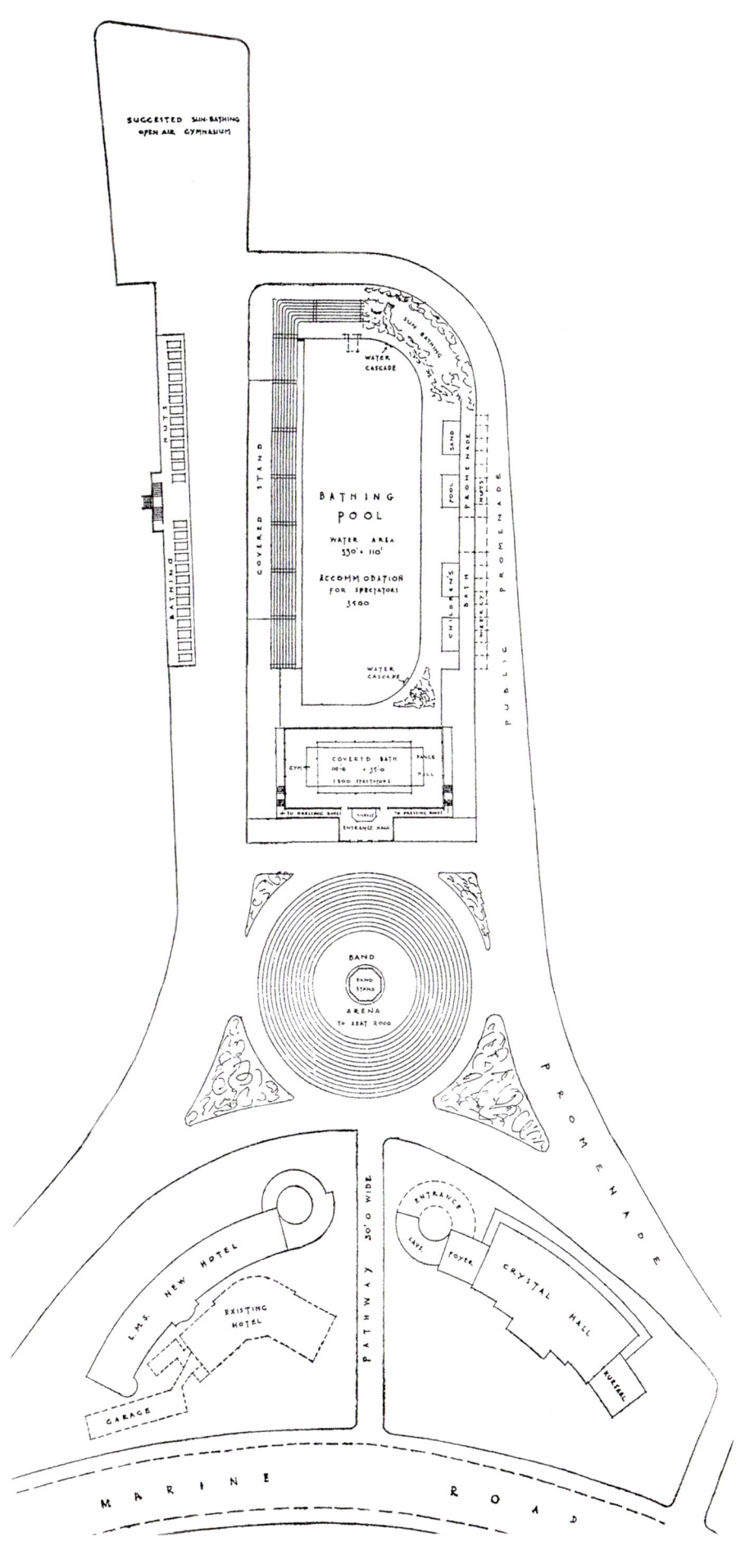

Plan of the Old Harbour Development Scheme prepared by the Borough Surveyor (Mr. R.B. Savage, M.I.M.C.E.).

and adjacent land for £57,000 was signed by the LMS and Morecambe Corporation. The Corporation immediately set about drawing up ambitious plans for their transformation. These were developed in detail over the following year by Mr R.B. Savage, the Borough Surveyor, and members of the Old Harbour Committee chaired by Councillor F.C. Fahy. When the plans were revealed to the public in January 1933 there was astonishment at the size and scope of the project.

The *Visitor* could not contain its enthusiasm, claiming the scheme would 'bring to Morecambe an era of prosperity such as few had ever dreamed of'. Letting its imagination off the leash, it conjured up a vision of the future for its readers. 'Fine buildings and lovely gardens will rise out of scrap heaps and waste land. The mud of the untidy harbour basin will be replaced by swimming pools and sunbathing terraces. The din of the shipbreakers' hammers and cranes will give way to the music of bands, and the merry splashing of bathers will be heard instead of the mournful lapping of waves round the hulks of doomed ships.'

Central to the overall scheme was the inclusion of a covered and heated pool situated at the landward end of the harbour basin. Fitted with a glass and steel roof which could be opened on warm days it was designed to accommodate 1,500 spectators. The Old Harbour Committee's decision was based on the belief that covered baths were profitable while open-air baths lost money. Swimming could take place all year round and provide children with more opportunities to learn to swim for, as one concerned councillor observed: "Although Morecambe is a seaside town only a small proportion of the children in it can swim." Occupying most of the original basin would be a considerably larger open-air pool, although this would initially be deferred and might be abandoned altogether if the covered pool proved sufficient to meet the demands for bathing. If this transpired, the space would be used as a sports stadium which could host a variety of events.

At the end of the Stone Jetty an area was set aside for sunbathing and as an open-air gymnasium. The Committee had noted the growing popularity of sunbathing for health reasons and attached almost as much importance to its provision as to swimming. There would be no restrictions with regard to mixed bathing, either in the sun or in the pool. For visitors preferring to swim in the sea, a long row of bathing huts in the style of Swiss chalets was planned for the south side of the jetty with access to the beach via steps. These would be equipped with toilets and hired out weekly or for the season.

Following a similar curve to that of the new Midland Hotel and almost mirroring its appearance was the proposed Crystal Hall. A circular entrance would lead to a foyer giving access to the main concert hall housing a small light orchestra in the season. This would have seating for 2,500 people and could be divided up by folding partitions to offer flexibility of accommodation for different activities. The main roof would be constructed almost entirely of glass. On the seaward side of the hall there would be a promenade balcony and terrace and also a sun lounge with Vita-glass roof and windows. Part of the building would be used as a Kursaal spa and soda fountain. As the Crystal Hall's advocates stated: 'The more diversified a resort's attractions are in wet weather, the more popular it becomes, because our uncertain summers have always to be taken into account by the holidaymaker when deciding where to spend his vacation.'

Located between the Crystal Hall and the covered swimming pool would be a large, circular band arena, sunk below the promenade level thus sheltering the audience from the often strong sea breezes. Seats in tiers rising one above the other would be capable of accommodating some 2,500 spectators. Grandiose in its conception, the planned transformation of the Old Harbour site was costed at £147,800. When a further £57,000 for a new sea wall and promenade was added on, the total reached an eye-watering £204,800.

Morecambe Corporation's next step was to submit its scheme to the Ministry of Health, the Government department responsible for scrutinising applications for loans in order to ensure that ratepayers' money was spent prudently. Forewarned that the Ministry might be reluctant to sanction such a large amount, the Borough Surveyor and Mr C.A. Mackay (Advertising Manager) decided to take another look at the plans and found that a considerable sum could be saved if the proposed promenade around the Old Harbour was re-aligned to run from the landward end of the Stone Jetty in a straight line to the Central Paddling Pool before curving inland to join the existing promenade. This would enclose a large area of the foreshore and provide a more accessible site on which to build the covered bath. They estimated that this amended scheme would reduce the cost by £36,000 and, as it would create more land (just over five acres/two hectares), certain attractions not in the original scheme could now be included. Among these were gardens, public walks, a café lounge and tea gardens, extra sunbathing facilities and the first wave bath in the British Isles. Even with these new features there would still be a saving of £20,600. The *Visitor* supported this revision as, in its opinion: 'Not only is it cheaper than the original one but it includes more attractions, reclaims a bigger area of the shore, gives more land for development and covers up one of the ugliest and most disreputable sections of the foreshore along Morecambe's sea front.'

In early April 1933 Morecambe Corporation passed the amended scheme with a large majority. Councillor Fahy said he had been in contact with the Ministry of Health since the beginning and was optimistic that approval would be given in due course. It was not unusual for Government departments to take their time in their deliberations but as spring drifted into summer and nothing had been heard from the Ministry, councillors and ratepayers were starting to get restive. Several councillors were implacably opposed to the Crystal Hall, unconvinced of its viability, and believed that the hold-up was due to the fact that the Ministry was not blind to the losses sustained by such buildings in other parts of the country. Even the *Visitor* conceded that the Ministry might be willing to accelerate the scheme if the Corporation offered to temporarily withdraw or abandon altogether the Crystal Hall.

The first hint of a decision came at the end of August when Morecambe's deputy mayor, Alderman J.C. Wilson, speaking after the Cross Bay Swim, mentioned that there was a possibility that the Ministry would request modification of the scheme. He said it was very likely that "with regard to the present costly scheme for a covered swimming pool, the Ministry will put serious objection to the spending of £80,000 on this and probably we shall have to have an outdoor pool". When the Ministry's report was published a few weeks later the deputy mayor's forecast proved to have been accurate. It had concluded that although the revised scheme for the Old Harbour site had shaved over £20,000

THE OLD HARBOUR SCHEME (REVISED)

	£
Sea Wall and Promenade surrounding site	21,000
(a) Storage and settling tanks under Promenade	2,500
(b) Repairs to existing stone harbour wall	1,500
(c) Improvement of wooden jetty	2,000
Covered Bath	80,000
Crystal Hall and Kursaal	30,000
(a) Lay-out of gardens, etc., surrounding Crystal Hall	1,000
Open air band enclosure and bandstand	6,000

Additional Items to complete the development of the land:-

Solarium	4,000
Public Conveniences	3,000
Lay-out of Stone Jetty	8,000
Bathing Chalets	3,000
Paddling Pool and walk on west side of Stone Jetty	2,000
Medicated Russian and Turkish Baths	7,300

Additional amenities possible on account of the increased area of land enclosed by sea wall in new scheme:-

Gardens, public walks, provision for sun bathing and small out-door wave bath	8,400
Café lounge and tea gardens	4,500

TOTAL £184,200

from the original estimate, it was still far too expensive and that approval would not be forthcoming unless the Corporation made further and far-reaching economies. The report suggested that much of the required saving could be achieved by opting for an open-air swimming pool rather than a covered one, pointing out that the cost of the latter and its surroundings alone would be about half the present rateable value of the Borough, which was a 'formidable proposal'. With this in mind, it recommended revisiting the original plan by the architects Cross & Sutton which would provide a pool roughly four times as large as the covered one and cost approximately half as much.

Having little choice but to take the Ministry's advice, the Old Harbour Committee proceeded to amend its amended scheme, managing to reduce the total by almost a third. Adopting an open-air pool would save around £35,000 while another £25,000 reduction could be achieved by cutting out the sunbathing solarium, medicated Russian and Turkish baths, café lounge and tea gardens, wave bath and bathing chalets. Although the Crystal Hall was still included, it was to be deferred indefinitely and such was the hostility towards it that the *Visitor* observed: 'To judge from the attitude of the Town Council, the Crystal Hall may be regarded as dead and done with.' The changes resulted in a revised total of £121,000, a figure which, to the Corporation's relief, finally proved acceptable to the Ministry. After a roller-coaster ride since the architectural competition in 1927, with ambitious and often unrealistic plans coming and going, the scheme appeared to be back where it started, in essence not unlike the original proposal of six years earlier. The crucial difference, however, was the securing of funding for a new sea wall and promenade which, when completed, would create a basin large enough to accommodate Cross & Sutton's design.

With approval achieved, the construction of the sea wall now became the Corporation's top priority. By a timely coincidence this tied in with another of its projects – the removal of a large mound known as Battery Hill, next to the Pleasure Park, in order to create suitable building land adjacent to Marine Road. The earth being excavated

An excavator at work on the removal of Battery Hill next to the Pleasure Park. Part of the Figure 8 railway can be seen behind the truck. The levelled site would later be occupied by the Empire Theatre and Cinema, Lunn's Arcade, Floral Hall and the Arcadian Pavilion.

Concrete supports for the new sea wall and promenade line the edge of the foreshore. The first section near the Stone Jetty has been reinforced with earth brought from Battery Hill.

from the site was mainly marl which was ideal material for backing up the sea wall and promenade. Prior to this happening a new concrete culvert had to be laid to lengthen the existing one which discharged sewage into the sea. As part of the work the original section, of rubble construction, should have been replaced with similar concrete pipework but was only patched up, a cost-saving decision that would turn out to have far-reaching consequences.

Ferro-concrete specialists Messrs Mouchel and Partners were given the contract to build the wall and construction started in earnest towards the end of 1934. Work went on twenty-four hours a day with acetylene flares used to illuminate the site at night, although they were limited in scope and often the wagons were tipping their loads in almost total darkness. Nevertheless, the job continued apace and in early April 1935 the *Visitor* was able to report that 'the recent fine weather has enabled considerable progress to be made in the construction of the surrounding sea wall and only a small gap remains before the site for the baths is enclosed. It is anticipated that the actual construction of the Bathing Pool will be commenced by the middle of April'.

The likelihood of this happening quickly evaporated when it was discovered that seepage of water into the basin was occurring where the sea wall had been built over the join between the old and new culverts. Attempts to plug the leak were proving unsuccessful and Mr L.D. Dodds, the consulting engineer of Mouchel and Partners, believed that water would continue to enter the basin unless the culvert was diverted. The Corporation said it would address the problem by building a replacement, skirting the adjacent paddling pool to link up with the new section of culvert on the seaward side of the wall but this would have to be delayed until September so as not to interfere with the holiday season. Despite these assurances the contractors for the swimming pool, Sir Lindsay Parkinson & Sons Ltd, stated they were not prepared to take possession of the site until the sea wall had been sealed and the basin was perfectly dry. However, after threats of legal action by the Corporation, Sir Lindsay reluctantly agreed to begin work. The leakage continued to be a problem throughout construction, the water only being kept at bay first by Corporation pumps and later by a bespoke pumping station.

By October the site had been sufficiently prepared for building to commence. On a grey and overcast autumn day 'on a platform a-flutter with gay pennants of bunting' the mayor of Morecambe, Alderman Thomas Waite, prepared to lay the foundation stone for the town's new swimming pool. In attendance were the mayors of Lancaster, Southport and Barrow, Sir Lindsay Parkinson, the architects Kenneth Cross and Cecil Sutton and assorted civic dignitaries. Councillor F.C. Fahy, chairman of the Old Harbour Committee, handed the mayor a glass container in which were a set of stamps and coins commemorating the Silver Jubilee of King George V, a copy of Morecambe's Official Guide and the current issue of the *Visitor* and other papers as a record of local news. This was set in a bed of cement and placed under the foundation stone which was gently lowered into place. Cecil Sutton then passed the mayor an oak and silver mallet with which he tapped the stone and declared it "well and truly laid". The granite block bore the inscription

Laying the foundation stone of the new Baths.

> THIS FOUNDATION STONE
>
> was laid by
>
> HIS WORSHIP THE MAYOR
>
> ALDERMAN THOMAS WAITE J.P.
>
> 7th OCTOBER 1935

The ceremony was followed by a luncheon at the Town Hall at which Kenneth Cross recalled that his firm's design for the Swimming Baths back in 1927 had been chosen by Morecambe Corporation. He had hoped at the time that the plans would be drawn in a few weeks, the baths started in a few months and the whole scheme completed in a year or eighteen months. Despite having to wait for eight years, he said: "We have never been downhearted and realised the difficulties that have been in the way. Happily, the completion of the scheme is now no longer a question of years, but of months."

HEALTH ABOUNDS

THREE

In the eight and a half years that had elapsed between the design competition for Morecambe's new swimming pool and the laying of its foundation stone nearly one hundred open-air pools/lidos had been built in England. Of these around a quarter were at seaside locations, the majority, not surprisingly, along the warmer south coast, from Penzance in Cornwall to Margate in Kent.

North-West England saw three contrasting lidos completed in this period – at Southport (1928), across Morecambe Bay at Grange-over-Sands (1932) and at New Brighton (1934). While Southport's large pool was not dissimilar in appearance to the one at Blackpool, and Grange Lido, tucked into the sea front, was relatively small, New Brighton's was in a different league altogether.

Located at the end of the Wirral peninsula, it was not only the largest open-air pool in the country but also set new standards for lido design. In a reaction to the neo-classical influences seen at earlier pools, New Brighton adopted the clean lines of a radical architectural style that was filtering through to Britain from the Continent, one which would later become known as *Art Deco*. Summarised by one writer as 'white-walled, flat-roofed and streamlined' and often complemented by decorative additions such as geometric motifs and abstract patterns, the style was ideally suited to lidos. New Brighton's early experimentation in Modernism, in which its main entrance block and two-tiered pavilion overlooking the pool were rendered in white 'snowcrete' highlighted by bands of green tiles, would be taken up by other seaside resorts and result in many of the finest lidos of the 1930s.

During this time the building of lidos was actively supported by the Government in the belief that exercise (swimming), fresh air and sunshine were helpful in promoting both physical and mental fitness. Research in Europe after the First World War had shown that sunlight was an important source of Vitamin D and could be used to combat a number of medical conditions, particularly tuberculosis. In 1923 Dr Auguste Rollier published *Heliotherapy*, an influential book outlining his methods for the treatment of the disease at his clinic in the Swiss Alps, using both natural sunlight and sunlamps.

In a remarkable *volte face* acquiring a suntan became fashionable. For centuries it had been the mark of a manual labourer, out in all weathers; the upper classes prized a pale

The word lido is derived from the Latin 'litus' meaning shore and was 'borrowed' from the beach resort of that name in Venice. While difficult to define precisely, it signifies more than just an open-air swimming pool and typically includes other amenities such as a sunbathing area and a café.

The lido, epitomised by Morecambe's Super Swimming Stadium, conjured up its own exciting atmosphere. The young, mingling on the sun terraces, revelled in the chance to show off their toned bodies while enjoying the benefits of sunlight on skin. Attitudes were changing from those expressed by a local councillor in 1934 who found 'the bathing and sunbathing on the beach … a disgrace to the town' to one where the Corporation promoted bathing as 'a healthy and joyous pastime' and Morecambe itself as a place where 'no annoying restrictions are imposed to mar one's happiness'.

skin, indicating a comfortable life led indoors. All this changed with celebrities such as Coco Chanel flaunting a tan that spoke of the glamour of Continental society. A new snobbery developed – maintaining a tan through winter suggested wealth, health and abundant leisure. In the summer sunshine, however, everyone could emulate this lifestyle, even if for only a few precious days each year.

Clothing began to reflect the growing popularity of outdoor activities. Women wore knee-length shorts to go hiking and the Women's League of Health and Beauty performed their open-air gymnastic displays in a fetching uniform of white satin sleeveless blouses and brief black shorts. In the swimming pool the change was equally revolutionary; costumes became much more like those of today in response to the demands of freedom while swimming and the desire to expose more skin to gain that all-important suntan.

For men, the shorts became shorter and sleeves were replaced by straps until, eventually, it became acceptable to bathe in trunks. For women, rubber caps worn over shorter hairstyles and briefer, more streamlined swimsuits allowed them to swim properly for the first time. In 1929 the firm of Jantzen produced a one-piece costume that was advertised as 'the suit that changed bathing into swimming'. The development of new materials in the 1930s (lighter, stretchy and less absorbent) gave rise to figure-hugging swimwear, focusing attention on an athletic body. Many of the railway posters of the era used the image of a swimsuit clad young female to highlight the attractions of the resorts they were advertising.

Concerns with public health and fitness also had a noticeable influence on lido design, requiring architectural structures to accommodate a variety of activities, from swimming and diving to sunbathing and spectating, as well as housing settling tanks, filtration and chlorination plants, plus changing rooms, showers and toilets, not forgetting the essential café. New construction techniques and building technologies, including steel frames and reinforced concrete, led to many lidos incorporating Modernist features – clean lines, flat roofs, and extensive use of glass and reflective surfaces, all of which, according to historian Fred Gray, 'enabled the open-air pool and lido … to become the pre-eminent architectural symbol of the British seaside in the first half of the twentieth century'.

What may seem strange is why lidos were so popular in seaside towns – if holidaymakers wanted to swim, what was wrong with the sea? Even odder was the fact that most lidos were built close to or on the seafront while some, like the Jubilee Pool at Penzance and Tinside Lido at Plymouth, were virtually in the sea. Perhaps it was because at some resorts bathers were required to pay for changing facilities such as cubicles or tents; a few councils even charged for bathing itself. Plus, of course, it was not easy to swim when the tide was out unless, as at Morecambe, one didn't mind a long-distance walk to reach the water. A lido enabled swimming at any time of the day, was often cheaper and offered a range of facilities. Crucially, thanks to its filtration systems, it was also cleaner and, in contrast to the sea, there was considerably less likelihood its patrons would be accompanied by floating items of sewage.

In their own way lidos captured the zeitgeist of the late 1920s and 1930s. Places for leisure and enjoyment certainly, but also beneficial to health and well-being – modern emblems of a brighter future and forerunners of a more egalitarian society, where everyone was welcome regardless of age, class and gender.

The hiatus since they won the competition for Morecambe's open-air pool in 1927 had provided Kenneth Cross and Cecil Sutton with the time and opportunity to reassess their original plans, not only in the light of developments in lido design during this period, but also in response to another significant event – the appearance of the LMS Railway's new Midland Hotel on Morecambe's seafront, little more than a stone's throw from the site for the town's swimming stadium. Designed by Oliver Hill and opened in July 1933 to unanimous acclaim, here was a stunning example of the latest architecture landing right on their doorstep like an alien spacecraft, and one that was impossible to ignore. Sparkling white in the sunlight, its flat-roofed, elegantly curvaceous form was the epitome of modernity and quite unlike anything seen before in an English seaside resort, its presence undoubtedly influencing Cross and Sutton in the amendments they would make to their design for the stadium.

Whilst retaining the basic rectilinear shape with its curved ends, they made several structural and aesthetic alterations. Out went the superfluous, and now passé, domes on the roofs of the entrance building and on the four corner blocks. Out also went the two sunken tennis courts at the front, to be replaced by ornamental gardens and pathways. In came a complete remodelling of the seaward side of the stadium, incorporating tiered banks of seating for spectators separated by a two-storey café in the modern style, plus the inclusion of a multi-level diving tower and well in the north-west corner.

By the mid-1930s reinforced concrete was increasingly being used for similar projects and Cross and Sutton adopted this as the principal building material for the stadium. The entrance block, café and concourses would be of beam and slab construction with

An image of the 'New Baths Scheme' taken from the brochure of the construction firm of Sir Lindsay Parkinson & Sons Ltd and reproduced on a postcard by Matthews of Bradford. It shows the proposed stadium gleaming in the sunlight with an ocean liner and a somewhat incongruous naval warship riding in the bay! Interestingly, the card was posted on 10th February 1936, nearly six months before the stadium actually opened, its sender writing: 'Some day we must come and visit this place and see the new Swimming Bath. Also go on a trip on one of the boats (top left hand corner of picture) on the new services they are running to Blackpool, Douglas and Belfast.'

Completion of the new sea wall and promenade enabled construction work in the basin to proceed irrespective of the state of the tide, with the curving western section of the stadium the first to take on a recognisable appearance.

mild steel reinforcement to the concrete. Upper floors, roofs and the terraced seating would all be supported on reinforced concrete columns. Brick, however, remained the architects' preferred option for the stadium's outer walls. These would be coated in cement render and painted white to create a more contemporary look in order to harmonise with its near neighbour which itself had been built in a similar way. In this respect, both the Midland Hotel and the Swimming Stadium flattered to deceive, their Modernism being only skin deep in places.

Late autumn was not the ideal time to begin work on a major building project. The days were shortening and the coming months were likely to be accompanied by a deterioration in the weather. Unfortunately for the contractors this proved to be the case. The winter of 1935/6 was particularly cold and, unusually for Morecambe, there was heavy snowfall at the end of January causing work to be suspended. When the snow eventually melted, the whole basin was transformed into a sea of mud.

A further setback occurred when workmen were excavating the diving well. Digging down to the required depth of sixteen feet (five metres) they struck a patch of running sand and a spring from which water was constantly bubbling up into the well bottom. To solve the problem extra piling and layers of concrete were needed to hold back the water, resulting in an additional outlay of £2,500. When this was added to other unforeseen items of expenditure, such as those incurred by the constant pumping to keep the site dry and the reinforcing of a faulty section of the new sea wall, the overall cost of the scheme was creeping up towards £130,000.

Two mobile cranes rumble back and forth along specially laid rail tracks as the seaward side of the stadium takes shape. Work is progressing on the café block which is rising between the concrete tiers of the spectator stands. In the foreground a line of piling marks the edge of the diving well.

Sitting nonchalantly on a scaffolding pole these two workmen seem little troubled by Health and Safety considerations.

The famous illusionist Deveen, who was appearing at the Winter Gardens in April 1936, demonstrates how to fund the swimming stadium by conjuring up £120,000 out of a hat – the amount the project was estimated to be costing at the time.

Echoing the style of its close neighbour the Midland Hotel, the stadium nears completion with just the paving of the east terrace to finish off, plus the rendering of the brickwork to match the pristine white of the entrance building.

By March progress had slipped so far behind schedule that the *Visitor* was becoming concerned that the Baths might not be ready for the planned opening on July 27th. However, it expressed confidence that although 'there was still a great deal of work to do, the next three months, with better weather, longer days and double shifts, will see a remarkable transformation'. Fortunately, conditions did improve after Easter, eventually leading to the hottest summer Morecambe had experienced for thirty years with temperatures frequently exceeding 80°F (27°C). This helped the contractors recover some of the time lost, as did the longer hours of daylight, but what eventually made the difference was the Corporation's last minute decision to employ extra labour and pay overtime rates to ensure that the building would be completed on time. In the end it was a close-run thing, but by the last week of July Morecambe's swimming stadium was finished and ready for the opening ceremony.

SUPERINTENDENT OF THE BATHS.

Mr. L. Flook, the Baths Superintendent, into whose care and keeping the great undertaking has been placed.

Leonard Flook took up his duties as Baths Superintendent at the beginning of July 1936 at a salary of £350 a year. He had previously held a similar position at New Ferry Baths in Bebbington on the Wirral.

WHAT'S IN A NAME?

As its new swimming pool was nearing completion, Morecambe Corporation decided to hold a competition to find an appropriate name, with a £5 prize for the winner. Hundreds of entries were sent in, including flights of fancy such as 'Friendship Harbour' and 'Utopian Joy Pool', while one man thought it should be called the 'Leo Pool' because Leo was the prevailing astrological sign on the date of the opening ceremony. All were rejected and the name chosen – the Super Swimming Stadium – was that suggested by the Corporation's own Advertising Manager, Harry Parker. Unfortunately for the luckless Harry, being an employee of the Corporation meant he was not eligible to claim the money.

Sir Josiah Stamp arrived early; it was 5.00am on July 27th when his personal train, equipped with sleeping accommodation, pulled into Morecambe's Promenade Station. As President of the London, Midland and Scottish Railway he had made the journey several times over the previous three years in order to visit the company's Midland Hotel but on this occasion it was at the request of Morecambe Corporation which had invited him to open its new swimming pool.

One of the most prominent public figures of the day, Sir Josiah was initially a civil servant, economist and businessman before becoming Chairman of the LMS in 1926. He served on several Royal Commissions and was also a director of the Bank of England. In 1918 he was awarded a CBE followed by a knighthood two years later before being raised to the peerage as Baron Stamp of Shortlands in Kent in 1938.

From the station it was only a short walk across Marine Road to the Midland Hotel where he would spend part of the morning putting the finishing touches to his speech which would be broadcast from the hotel prior to the opening ceremony. As the guests arrived they were directed to the hotel lawn where a marquee had been erected for a cocktail reception at which they were introduced to Sir Josiah by the mayor, Councillor Walter Townsley.

At one o' clock just over 150 people sat down to a luncheon of Canteloupe Melon, Cold Consommé, Mayonnaise of Salmon, Supreme of Chicken Janette with Japanese salad, Rainbow Ice and Coffee, the meal supervised by the hotel's popular Swiss manager Mr August. Joining Sir Josiah and Lady Ashton at the top table were the mayor and mayoress of Morecambe and Heysham and their counterparts from several northern towns and cities, including Leeds, Bradford, Manchester and Blackpool. Members and officers of Morecambe Corporation filled nearly half the dining room while the remaining tables were occupied by the architects and contractors of the stadium, officials from the LMS Railway Company, representatives of the Amateur Swimming Association, reporters from local and national newspapers, a dozen Justices of the Peace and sundry other local worthies. Lending a touch of glamour to this largely dark-suited gathering was Miss Doris Bower, the Cotton Queen of Great Britain, who was attending in her capacity as ambassadress for one of Lancashire's most important industries. Also among those dining were two of the workmen employed in building the stadium, chosen by ballot to attend the ceremony. While perhaps feeling a bit awkward in such company, they were as entitled as anyone to be there, probably more so than most.

In his speech, which was relayed by loudspeakers to the waiting crowd, Sir Josiah outlined his long association with Morecambe and praised the Corporation for its initiative. "I cannot think of any corresponding cause anywhere in the country where there has been as much new thought and imagination in the last ten years. Your present council and its administration seem to be constantly engaged in putting 'More' into Morecambe. I see that apt alliteration's artful aid, which produced 'Britain's Bonniest Bay', has now evolved 'Super Swimming Stadium'. If that doesn't fetch 'em from Bradford and all other places, I don't know what will." To the amusement of his audience he pondered on his invitation to open the swimming pool. "Whether I have any right or qualification for taking part in today's ceremony I don't know. My recent entry as a member of the

The mace bearer and the mayor and mayoress of Morecambe lead a winding crocodile of guests along the promenade from the Midland Hotel to the Swimming Stadium. Sir Josiah Stamp is behind the mayor and Lady Ashton and slightly to the left. Hours before the ceremony a huge crowd had gathered, stretching through the Harbour Gardens, along the Promenade, past the Midland Hotel and almost as far as the Astoria Cinema nearly half a mile away. It soon became obvious that the numbers waiting to get into the stadium far exceeded its capacity, a fact which seemed to be realised by a section of the crowd who made a sudden rush for the entrance. To avert a potentially dangerous situation the doors were immediately closed and a decision made not to admit any more spectators even though there was still space.

honourable Order of the Bath may have something to do with it. The motto of that great Order is 'Three joined in one' and I am entitled to assume in this case that it means Morecambe and Heysham and the LMS."

On a more serious note Sir Josiah stated: "Your new bath is not only the last word in modernity, but it also gives the facilities for a recreation and sport which will stay with us always. Bathing and swimming is a great feature of modern life, yet it isn't a hundred years since it was the privilege and joy of only a few. Today, bathing reduces rich and poor, high and low, to a common standard of enjoyment and health. When we get down to swimming, we get down to democracy. This pool will not provide only pleasure, but is a great contribution to the health of the nation."

Other speeches followed after which the guests walked in procession to the swimming stadium along the new promenade which had been temporarily closed to the public. Behind the barriers dense crowds of people lined the route. The ceremony itself was short and simple. The speeches having already taken place, Sir Josiah formally opened the baths by switching on the cascade from which a spout of water bubbled up and streamed into the pool. "With every good wish for the prosperity of Morecambe and Heysham I have much pleasure in declaring open this swimming pool."

In commemoration of the event Sir Josiah was presented with a silver bowl by the Corporation and with a cigarette box by the architects. Councillor F.C. Fahy, Chairman of the Old Harbour Committee, received a silver model of the swimming stadium, and the mayor a silver salver, both from the contractors. To christen the pool three members of Southport's Albatross Diving Club made the first plunge into the water, one from each of the diving boards. This was followed by a display of high and fancy diving, exhibition swimming and mannequin parades, all accompanied by incidental music provided by Foden's Motor Works Band. With the conclusion of the entertainment the crowd dispersed, Sir Josiah departed in his private train and the stadium staff set to work cleaning up the pool and its surroundings ready for its reopening for public bathing that evening.

It had, the *Visitor* concluded, been a momentous day for the resort. 'The Bath will make Morecambe's popularity grow enormously. It has been sorely needed. Every ratepayer with any knowledge of the holiday-making public knows that lack of bathing facilities has lost to the town each year thousands of visitors – particularly the young, free-spending type.' To celebrate the opening the *Visitor* printed an unprecedented 12,000 copies of its normal edition, plus a separate four-page pictorial supplement at a cost of 2d, twice the price of the regular newspaper.

Perhaps it was just a coincidence, but that week the town's Palladium Cinema was showing a science-fiction film set in the near future and based on the H.G. Wells novel *The Shape of Things to Come*.

Borough of Morecambe and Heysham

Programme

of the Opening

of the

Open Air Bathing Pool

by

Sir Josiah Stamp, G.C.B., G.B.E.

Monday, 27th July, 1936.

Programme of the opening ceremony of the Super Swimming Stadium on 27th July 1936.

Order of Proceedings

12-0 noon — Guests will proceed to the Midland Hotel for the reception by His Worship the Mayor of Morecambe and Heysham (Councillor W. Townsley, J.P.) at the head of the steps leading to the front lawn.

12-30 p.m. — Luncheon at the Midland Hotel.

2-15 p.m. — Proceed from the Midland Hotel along the promenade to the Bathing Pool and via the main entrance to the reserved enclosure on the Central Terrace.

2-30 p.m. — The Mayor will request Sir Josiah Stamp to commence the circulation of the water by turning on the cascade and formally declare the Morecambe and Heysham Open Air Bathing Pool open.

Presentations to

Sir Josiah Stamp, G.C.B., G.B.E., by the Corporation
"Tazza" Bowl.

Sir Josiah Stamp, G.C.B., G.B.E., by the Architects
Cigarette Box.

The Chairman of the Old Harbour Committee (Councillor F. C. Fahy, J.P.) by the Contractors.
Silver Replica of the Bath.

His Worship the Mayor (Councillor W. Townsley, J.P.) by the Contractors
Silver Salver.

The succeeding programme of aquatic events will include:

Mannequin Parades by the "Windsor" Water Woollie Girls.

High and Fancy Diving by the Scott Brothers and Messrs. Gore and Partner.

Exhibition Swimming by Miss Lucy Morton and Members of the Lancaster and Morecambe and Heysham Amateur Swimming Associations.

Incidental Music by Foden's Motor Works Band
Bandmaster—F. Mortimer.

The Pool will be open to the public at 6-30 p.m.

Silver model of the Super Swimming Stadium and its dedication.

PRESENTED TO

COUNCILLOR FRANCIS CHARLES FAHY J.P.

CHAIRMAN OF THE OLD HARBOUR COMMITTEE OF THE MORECAMBE
AND HEYSHAM TOWN COUNCIL

ON THE OCCASION OF THE OPENING OF THE OPEN-AIR BATHING POOL 27th JULY 1936

BY THE CONTRACTORS

MESSRS. SIR LINDSAY PARKINSON & CO. LTD. OF BLACKPOOL

ARCHITECTS – MESSRS. CROSS AND SUTTON. 45 & 46 NEW BOND STREET. LONDON. W.1.

Viewed from the terrace in the north-west corner, an unusual stillness pervades the finished stadium, as if awaiting the crowds to bring it to life.

MORECAMBE & HEYSHAM
OPEN AIR BATHING POOL

THE —
SUPER SWIMMING STADIUM
IS NOW OPEN DAILY
7-0 A.M. TO 9-0 P.M.

Special Floodlight Sessions, 10 p.m. to Midnight as occasion demands.

SCALE OF CHARGES

ADULT BATHERS	6d.
,, PROMENADERS	6d.
JUNIOR BATHERS	4d.
,, PROMENADERS	4d.
BOOKS OF TICKETS purchased in advance,	15 Tickets for 5/-
CLUB SEASONS	7/6

(Available only on production of the Morecambe and Heysham A.S.A. Membership Receipt.)

L. FLOOK, Baths Superintendent.   Telephone 1018

PEACE AND WAR

FOUR

The first weekend after the opening of the Super Swimming Stadium was that of the August Bank Holiday and huge crowds were expected in the resort. Over the three days of the holiday tens of thousands of visitors poured into Morecambe by rail and road – and rain poured down on the visitors. Worse weather for the newly opened swimming pool could scarcely have been imagined. However, despite having to endure temperatures more like November than August, most people seemed determined to enjoy themselves and, as the *Visitor* observed: 'Overcoated, mackintoshed and umbrella'd, they braved the torrents of rain and boisterous, blustery winds.' Given the circumstances, it was remarkable that several thousand holidaymakers paid for admission to the swimming stadium during the three day weekend. Not surprisingly, only the hardiest fancied bathing in such cold conditions and it was estimated that fewer than 15% of customers actually ventured into the water. 'Installation of a heating plan may again be considered by the Town Council in view of this', opined the *Visitor*.

It is more than likely that many of those paying the 6d entry fee (4d for children) did so just to take a closer look at Morecambe's spectacular new swimming pool. Measuring 396 feet (121 metres) by 110 feet (34 metres), it was certainly impressive. Although not the largest in the country – that distinction still belonged to New Brighton's lido – it was the longest by six feet (1.8 metres). The pool had a capacity of 1,250,000 gallons with water drawn directly from the open sea into a settling tank below the terraced grandstands. From here it was pumped at high pressure through a filtration plant where it was cleaned and sterilised before entering the pool via six inlets and a tiered cascade, the whole volume being circulated every 6½ hours.

Concerned by a campaign the *Daily Mail* had been running against 'unhealthy swimming baths', Morecambe Corporation sought to reassure the public that its new pool would be free from any such criticism, claiming that the water would be cleaner than the water supply of any town in the kingdom. 'It will be fit to drink – except it won't taste so nice because it will be sea-water.' The depth of water in the pool varied from virtually nothing to 6 feet 6 inches (2 metres), with a 16 feet (5 metres) deep well at the base of the diving tower.

It is interesting to note that while imperial units for measurement were the norm in Britain at the time, in order to comply with international competition regulations,

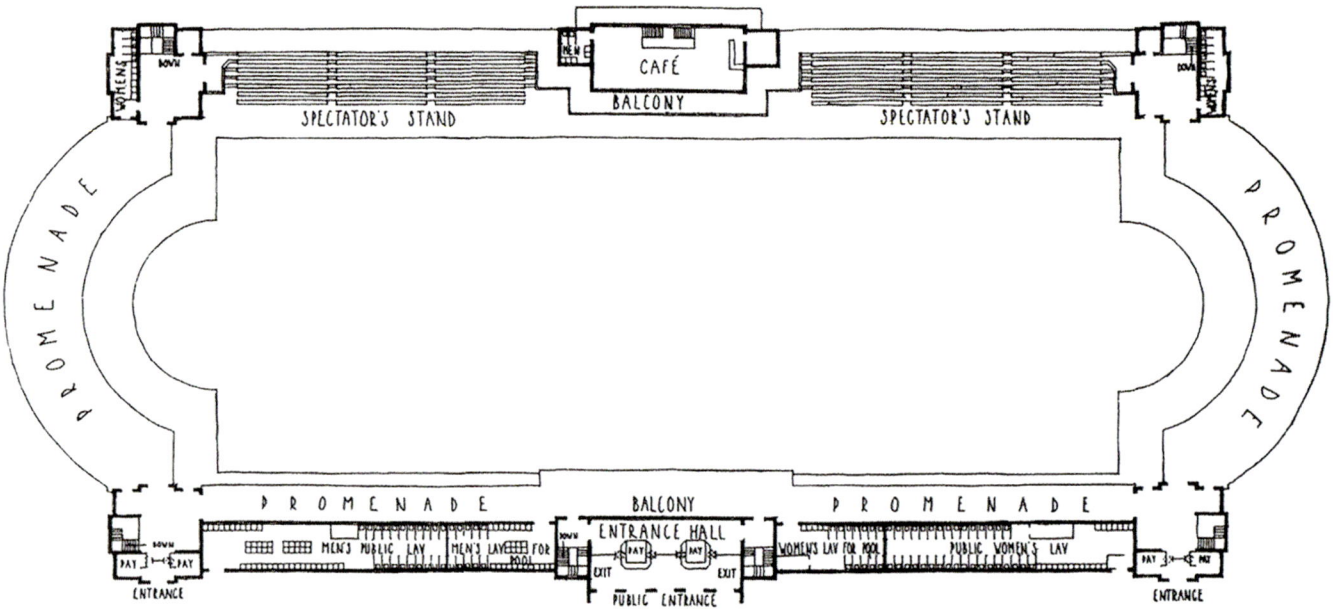

Plan of the Super Swimming Stadium.

diving boards in swimming pools had to be at specific metric heights. Thus on the diving tower there were boards at three, five and ten metres, plus separate springboards at one and three metres.

On entering the stadium through the main turnstiles bathers would pass into the entrance hall and descend stairs to pool level where the dressing and locker rooms were located. These were strictly segregated, men to the left and women to the right. Having changed into their swimming costumes they then had to walk through a pre-cleansing system of showers and footbaths before being allowed to enter the pool. Also to be found on this level were the boiler house, laundry, offices and filtration plant.

There was ample room for non-bathers. Incoming spectators would cross the entrance hall onto a balcony overlooking the water. From here a walkway and spacious promenade ran in each direction, curving around the pool to reach two large tiered grandstands on the seaward side of the stadium. These were equipped with seating for 2,000 spectators, while sheltered colonnades at either end of the pool could each accommodate around 500 people in deckchairs. Refreshments were available from a two-storey café situated between the grandstands. Other facilities would be added later, including the Remedial Department which was accessed from the main entrance hall. Described as being 'beneficial, invigorating and pleasurable' the treatments comprised a Steam Cabinet, Foam Bath and Pine, Aeration and Seaweed Baths, plus various types of massage. On the opposite side of the entrance hall were committee rooms used for meetings and entertaining guests.

Because the stadium had not opened until the end of July and would close in September, the season was relatively short. The poor weather which had marred the Bank Holiday weekend continued on and off for the rest of August and there were many days on which the water in the swimming pool was too cold for bathing and the stadium was practically deserted; no bathers meant no spectators and, worryingly for the Corporation, no income. The obvious remedy was, as the *Visitor* had suggested, the installation of a heating system. North Lancashire was definitely not the Mediterranean but if the water in the pool could be maintained at a comfortable temperature fewer potential bathers might be dissuaded by inclement weather. Discussions took place over the winter months before a decision to proceed was reached. While most councillors were in favour, not everyone was convinced – it seemed a huge undertaking to heat a volume of 1,250,000 gallons of water to a planned temperature of around 70°F (21°C) and to maintain it at that level. No attempt to heat an open-air bath of such a size had ever been made before.

In March 1937 a scheme was announced to provide a gas-fired boiler at a cost of £700. The contract was awarded to Messrs Cochran & Company, Annan Ltd., working in co-operation with Morecambe Corporation's Gas Department. It was originally intended to have the system in operation by Whitsun but in early May Cochran's advised the Corporation that it was having difficulty in obtaining certain steel parts for the boiler. This delayed completion by over a month and it was not until July 9th that the machinery was switched on. 52 hours and £32 in gas later the water in the pool had reached the desired temperature. Morecambe could now claim the distinction of having the largest heated open-air swimming pool in the world. To ensure the public did not remain unaware of this latest innovation, the word HEATED was emblazoned in large capital letters over the stadium's main entrance.

With the heating system in place, the aim was to try to maintain an average water temperature of between 65°F and 67°F (19°C) which would provide 'delightful and comfortable bathing'. In theory, the cost of running the plant could be kept at a reasonable level because once the water had been heated it would hold its temperature for several days and the boiler could be turned off until a deterioration in the weather necessitated its restart. Attendances during the weekend after the heating was turned on more than vindicated the Corporation's decision to fund the project. Records were broken on the Sunday and emergency changing accommodation had to be brought into use. Large crowds became the norm in the days leading up to the August Bank Holiday which would prove to be in complete contrast to the washout of 1936. A combination of beautiful sunny weather and a heated pool attracted over 24,000 paying customers into the stadium on the Sunday and Monday, more than twice the number who had bought tickets the previous year.

Although the warmer water had helped to boost attendances, councillors were not slow to realise that an open-air pool which could be used only in the summer months would not generate sufficient income to repay the very large sum which the Corporation had borrowed to finance its construction. Money drained away as surely as the water at the end of the season. The solution was to persuade people to spend more when the stadium was open by offering something different to entice them in. If, as its name implied, it was to be a true stadium it would need to be a focus for entertainment and events as much as a place for swimming and sunbathing. The previous August, three weeks after the opening ceremony, a swimming gala had been held at the pool with admission prices of 1/- for adults and 6d for children. While heavy rain meant that

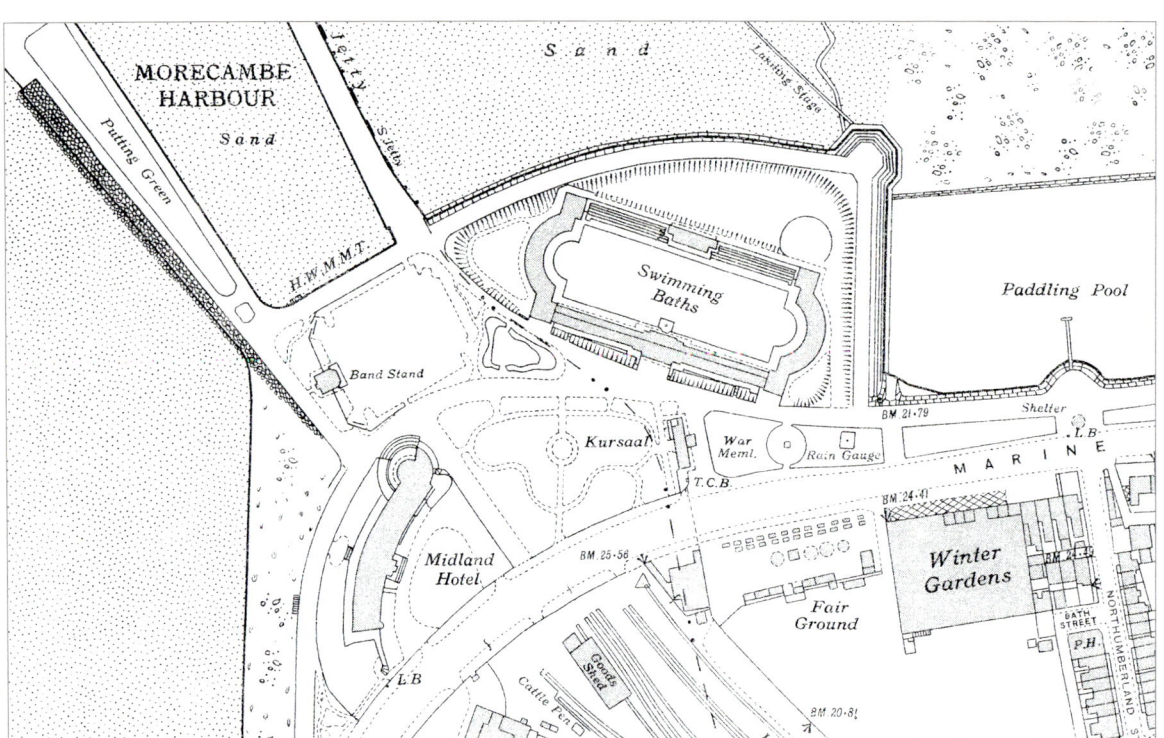

Ordnance Survey map of part of Morecambe's seafront in 1938.

The Super Swimming Stadium in its setting on Morecambe's seafront c1946, its curved ends echoing those of Oliver Hill's elegant Midland Hotel a short distance away. Between the two, in age as well as location, is the Harbour Band Arena which opened in 1934. From the start it proved extremely popular with holidaymakers and residents alike, with famous bands often playing to more than 2,000 people who filled the serried rows of deckchairs. For those preferring quieter surroundings there were ornamental gardens to wander and a little stream for children to paddle in or sail their model boats.

Once the site of Ward's shipbreakers, the nearby Stone Jetty now provides a seaward extension of the promenade. Its redundant wooden counterpart was eventually dismantled in 1948. Across Marine Road from the stadium, with facades in the *Art Deco* style, are the Littlewoods and Woolworths buildings, completed just before World War Two.

Aerial view of the Super Swimming Stadium the year after it opened. The sunken area between the building and the new promenade has been laid out with municipal-style flower beds rather than the 15-hole putting course that was originally envisaged. (A smaller, Crazy Golf attraction would later appear in the triangular space at the top of the picture.) The stadium itself is full of bathers, mostly spread over the shallower parts of the pool, with fewer in the swimming lanes. The deep water below the diving tower stands out as a dark rectangle. Spectators pack the two main grandstands either side of the café while sunbathers top up their tans on the upper terraces flanking the main entrance.

On a warm, sunny day the stadium is packed with people. A few serious swimmers use the lanes in the deeper part of the pool while the shallow end and side are thronged with children and less confident adults. As was usually the case, bathers are far outnumbered by spectators.

Light refreshments were available at the popular stadium café, managed in the early years by the Palatine Ice and Cold Supply Company of Blackburn on the basis of 10% of gross receipts. Its cantilevered balcony provided one of the best views of the pool. The low wall in front of the stands was designed to maintain cleanliness and hygiene by dissuading spectators from encroaching onto the pool surrounds.

In 'Kiddies Korner' the water was very shallow, providing a safe environment for small children and those content just to paddle.

Smiling children pose on the smaller of the stadium's two slides. Its big brother at the deep end of the pool (see front cover) descended 'with exhilarating abruptness' from a height of 14 feet (4.3 metres) into a depth of 4½ feet (1.4 metres) of water.

Curved colonnades at either end of the stadium provided semi-shaded areas where spectators could relax in deckchairs out of the direct glare of the sun – or shelter when it rained!

the 500 spectators got almost as wet as the competitors, the event made a modest profit and encouraged the Corporation to plan a more ambitious programme for the following year.

The 1937 season had opened on May 13th with free entry to the stadium, a gesture by the Corporation to help residents celebrate the Coronation of George VI. On June 8th the first event to be staged was a mannequin display by the girls of Windsor Water Woollies. If councillors had been apprehensive about its appeal to the public all doubts were dispelled as they watched 3,000 paying spectators pass through the turnstiles. The *Visitor*'s reporter seemed to have quite enjoyed the show. 'One by one the mannequins, attired in modern costumes of the most striking pattern and colour, strolled up and down the sides of the bath showing off the latest beach creations – creations which made feminine mouths water with envy. There were bathing suits of the latest Chromium Cellophane and Lastex yarn, and wool suits which appeared to be too good to wet with sea water. Red, white and blue were the predominant colours in all the parades. The comedy of the afternoon was provided by the parade of swimming costumes from 1870 to the present time.'

An even larger crowd of 7,000 people, over two sessions, paid £216 admission on July 14th to marvel at an exhibition of Olympic standard diving by Pete Desjardins from Miami, billed as 'The World's Greatest Artist of the Diving Stage', and Chicago based Marian Mansfield, 'America's Most Beautiful Diver'. Pete Desjardins' soubriquet was not undeserved as he had won both springboard and high diving gold medals at the Amsterdam Games in 1928. Marian Mansfield was also in the Olympic team and her demonstration of swimming strokes was considered 'instructive and entertaining'. Due to a deluge of rain, their performances the following day drew a disappointing total of barely 900 spectators.

In the summer of 1937 the stadium opened its doors to activities other than swimming. Here spectators are enjoying a parade of bathing costumes through the ages being modelled by mannequins from Windsor Water Woollies.

Arriving in Morecambe on July 26th for a stay of three days were eight ladies known as the Eugène Mermaids. They made up the first water ballet troupe in England, early precursors of the Aqualovelies who would grace the stadium's water shows in the 1950s and 1960s.

Bob Bradborn, 'The Canadian Lumberjack', entertained the crowds in the first week of September with demonstrations of log-rolling, not only balancing on a rotating log but, at the same time, skipping or reading a newspaper and drinking a cup of tea! The season ended with a prestigious swimming competition, the Northern Counties Mile Championship, at which the British record was broken by Norman Wainwright of Hanley, just edging out his close rival Robert Leivers of Longton, both of whom had competed in the Berlin Olympics the previous year.

In between the above events a number of swimming championships took place under the auspices of the Amateur Swimming Association, and the *Daily Chronicle* newspaper sponsored a 'Learn to Swim' campaign for children.

The Eugène Mermaids were England's first water ballet troupe. They travelled the country to promote Eugène of London's Permanent Wave hairstyling. One of their members was Ethel Lowry (back row centre) who had swum the English Channel in 1933.

After its winter break the stadium reopened in 1938 with Leonard Flook, the Baths Superintendent, assuring patrons that 'The Wonder Heating Apparatus' would again be in operation. Opening hours would normally be from 7am to 9pm, but from the first week in September, when the resort's Illuminations were on, closing time would be extended to 11pm. Entrance prices for bathers and spectators remained at 6d for adults and 4d for children, while books of 15 tickets cost 5/- and 3/- respectively. Reduced rates were available for members of the Morecambe and Heysham Amateur Swimming Association.

On June 8th spectators witnessed the first appearance in Britain of Tony Zukas and Frank Foster, 'America's Premier High, Fancy and Spectacular Divers'. Speaking after their performance Tony Zukas enthused that in ten years swimming and diving all over the world he had never known a bath to equal Morecambe's Super Swimming Stadium. "Everything is so clean and the temperature is perfect."

The season then settled into a similar pattern to that of 1937 with a mixture of swimming galas and special events designed to attract large audiences of non-bathing spectators. Opportunities were also provided for local divers and swimmers to display their skills for the public's entertainment. One of the first of these was Malcolm (Mac) Martin who had learned to dive growing up in Blackpool. After his family moved to Morecambe he spent long hours practising at the pool and teaching youngsters to dive until they were good enough to perform before an audience.

The year also brought the first criticism of the new heating system – one which might strike a chord with any reader who frequented the swimming stadium in their youth. In September a visitor from Leeds was less than happy that the water was colder than advertised, being chilly and uninviting despite the sun blazing down. "I was informed that the heating apparatus had been turned off earlier in the week and that it was practice to heat the water up to 72 degrees and then turn it off until the temperature was low enough to call for a further heating. How could the temperature of the water have been 66 degrees as advertised when the heater was not working and the atmosphere varied in temperature from day to day?" He urged the authorities to "keep faith with the public and give the visitor a fair deal". His was not a lone voice regarding the heating of the pool – or rather lack of it. Concerns were also raised at the Annual General Meeting of the Morecambe Amateur Swimming Club when younger members complained about the coldness of the water and were not convinced that the heating apparatus was working properly. Leonard Flook, the Baths Superintendent, who was at the meeting, revealed that the boiler had actually been turned off owing to the expense, adding that he was only following the Corporation's instructions and had no choice in the matter.

In 1939 the stadium opened on May 25th amid rumours of war. While aware of events unfolding in Europe, people still harboured hope that a conflict might be avoided and, in the meantime, were determined to enjoy themselves. The Whitsun holiday was blessed with glorious weather and record numbers of visitors flooded into Morecambe. Over the weekend 12,185 bathers and spectators frequented the stadium, nearly 2,000 more than the previous two Whitsuns combined.

Malcolm (Mac) Martin poised on the edge of the ten metre diving board, an image captured by the Matthews photographer and turned into a postcard, one of a series of the Super Swimming Stadium produced by the Bradford firm. This card belonged to Mac who signed and dated it. Sadly, his diving career was cut short by damaged ear-drums, a not uncommon complaint among high divers, and he retired to help run the family furniture business in Morecambe.

Mac Martin was also a keen body-builder and is shown here posing at the stadium.

A noteworthy event took place in July when the stadium hosted a 'Grand Beauty Parade' – a forerunner of the bathing beauty contests which would become synonymous with Morecambe after World War Two. This was a heat of the *Daily Dispatch* newspaper's quest for 'The Seaside Girl' and brought an entry of some 100 competitors in three different age classes: 4-9 years, 9-16, and 16+. The winner of the open class was 19-year old Fiona Plante of Tow Law, a domestic servant working in Morecambe, who qualified for the final of the competition. In the *Visitor*'s opinion: 'Seldom has the Super Swimming Stadium presented a more colourful spectacle than it did in Wednesday's brilliant sunshine when a bathing beauty parade was held. Summery frocks, colourful swimsuits and gay dressing gowns made the crowd of 9,000 people look like a human rainbow.'

By August the situation on the continent had worsened and in Morecambe the probability of war was uppermost in the minds of residents and holidaymakers alike. Both could not have failed to notice how Air Raid Precaution work had been stepped up as the authorities began to put their contingency plans into operation. While most other towns in the country were preparing black-out schemes, Morecambe was about to switch on its Illuminations. On Friday 25th August the famous radio gardening expert C.H. Middleton, watched by some 10,000 people crammed into the Harbour Band Arena, threw a switch and, in an instant, 'the town was transformed into a blaze of glittering, colourful light'.

For one of the set pieces of the Illuminations, a large and elaborate tableau had been constructed at the eastern end of the swimming pool depicting the court of the sea god Neptune who was seated on a chariot pulled by two prancing horses. Also in the stadium, a more topical note was struck by an air-raid mock-up consisting of a battery of searchlights on the café roof which criss-crossed the sky locating imaginary enemy planes. One by one the searchlights would 'spot' their target, 'anti-aircraft guns' would fire and 'hits' would be registered – a make-believe scenario that in the coming weeks would begin to be played out for real.

On Sunday 3rd September the official announcement came that Britain was at war with Germany. Many visitors cut short their stay, urged to return home by loudspeaker vans which toured the town's streets. Others chose to remain and finish their holiday, some even helping in A.R.P. work such as filling sandbags, and in the week after war was declared Morecambe was still very busy. A few days later came the introduction of a nationwide compulsory black-out and with it the cancelling of the Illuminations. The Government also ordered the closure of places of entertainment; cinemas, theatres, ballrooms, etc, were all shut down, as was the Super Swimming Stadium. Why it was included when bowling greens, tennis courts and the like remained open was, to many people, something of a mystery. However, once the Government began to realise the detrimental effect its decision was having on morale it moved quickly to rescind the decree.

From then on the swimming stadium continued to operate much as normal throughout the war years. The conflict had not meant the end of Morecambe as a holiday resort – if anything, the reverse was true. While many of the hotels and guest houses had

Bathers appear to be part of Neptune's kingdom as they congregate at the entrance to his seaweed-fringed grotto during the abruptly curtailed 1939 Illuminations season.

Seated on a chariot pulled by two horses led by bare-breasted nereids with flowing hair, Neptune holds his trident aloft while 'singing' "I am Neptune Lord of the Sea".

During its first year the stadium's opening times were usually from 7am to 9pm, with special late-night floodlight sessions put on 'as occasion demands'. The latter proved to be so popular that from 1937 they became a regular fixture every Monday, Wednesday, Thursday and Saturday evenings from 10.30pm till midnight 'when conditions are favourable'. The admission price of 1/- was twice that of the daily rate, presumably to cover the increase in overhead costs.

In these sessions the stadium took on an enchanted look. Lit by powerful floodlights and underwater lamps set into the sides of the pool, its transformed appearance was recorded in a series of atmospheric postcards called 'Reflections', three of which are shown here.

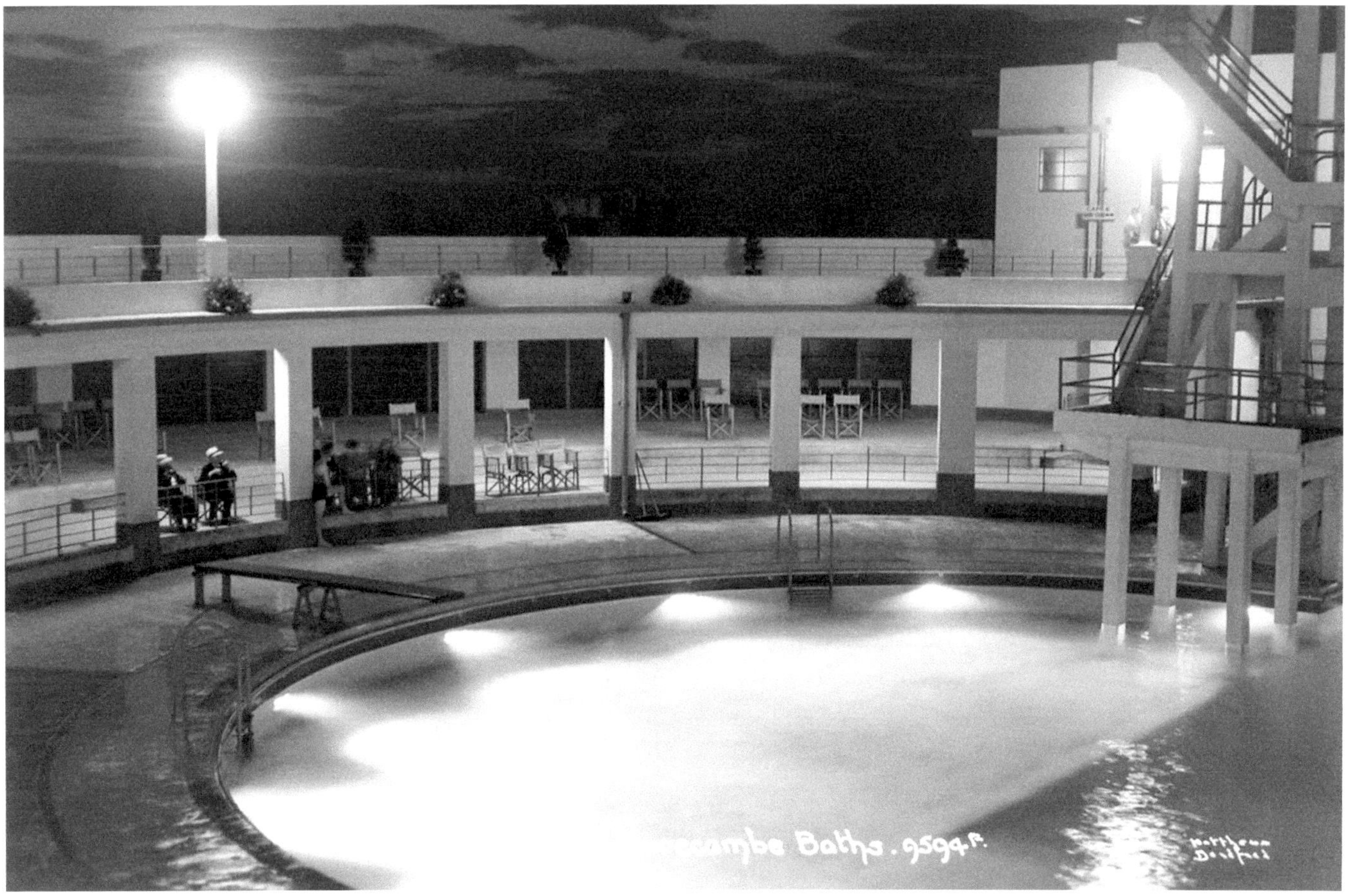
Baths . 9594 F.

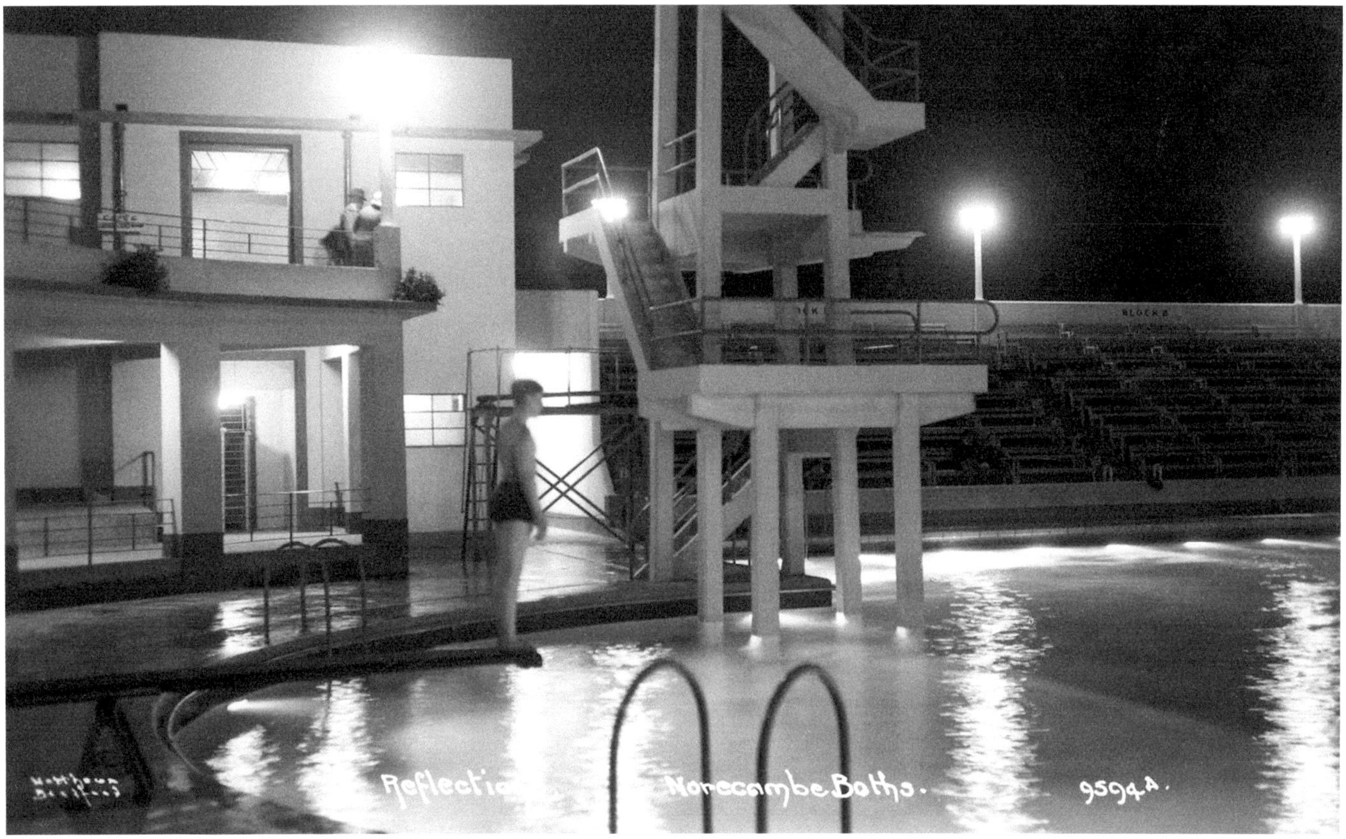
Reflectio
Morecambe Baths.
9594 A.

been requisitioned for civil servants (transferred from London) and for RAF recruits undergoing basic training in the resort, sufficient accommodation remained to cater for those holidaymakers keen to escape the privations of living in bomb-threatened towns and cities. Despite a national 'stay at home' campaign by the Government and the withdrawal of non-essential rail excursions, Morecambe enjoyed a series of successful wartime summers helped, no doubt, by its relatively safe geographical location.

Attendances at the stadium varied, usually higher on public holidays but very much dependent on the weather. In 1940 a hot and sunny August Bank Holiday saw it packed, with people queuing up to bathe. The next year, in complete contrast, Morecambe had its quietest August weekend since 1918, the wet and miserable conditions resulting in empty streets, windswept pavements and shuttered shops, and a virtually deserted swimming pool. Visitor numbers were also poor in 1942 thanks initially to a dismal Whitsun when the town attracted around a quarter of its normal peacetime total. Although conditions improved for the August Bank Holiday, only 3,215 paid for entrance to the stadium over the three days, a disappointingly low figure.

Better weather in the early part of the 1943 season drew some 30,000 visitors to Morecambe over the Whitsun weekend with numbers at the swimming pool nearly double those of the previous year. In late July the RAF staged a charity gala at the stadium which was loaned for the occasion free of charge by Morecambe Corporation. Around 6,000 spectators enjoyed an afternoon of competitive swimming and exhibition diving, the event raising £136 for the RAF Benevolent Fund.

As 1944 turned into 1945 the end of the war in Europe appeared tantalisingly in sight. In Morecambe an air of optimism pervaded the resort regarding the forthcoming holiday season. Having emerged virtually unscathed from the conflict, it was well placed to take advantage of people's desire to escape to the seaside to celebrate the end of hostilities, which they did in their tens of thousands following the surrender of Germany on May 8th.

In his office Leonard Flook was busy finalising his plans for the coming season. Two months earlier, as President, he had chaired the Annual General Meeting of the National Association of Baths Superintendents, the first time it had been held in Morecambe. Delegates gathered in the King's Arms to hear the deputy mayor, Councillor F. Clayton, extol the virtues of swimming which, he believed, "would play a great part in the life of the youth of the nation in the future", adding that "there was not any other exercise that was better fitted for physical development than swimming". Commenting on the design of modern open-air baths he noted that there had been much discussion as to whether the heating of such baths was a possibility. Referring to the Corporation's experience at the Super Swimming Stadium, he acknowledged that it was certainly possible but urged caution to any Council contemplating the installation of a heating system. "We found that, in practice, it could be done but we had found also that it incurred too great an expense to keep the water at anything like 60 degrees. It used too much gas and was not a paying proposition."

It was therefore no surprise to bathers that when the stadium opened for the 1945 season on May 17th they were greeted by a decidedly chilly swimming pool. What probably surprised them more was a 50% increase in admission charges, from 6d to 9d for adults and 4d to 6d for juniors, although prices for spectators remained unchanged. However, neither the water temperature nor the price rises seemed to deter those wishing to avail themselves of the stadium's attractions during that first summer of peace, so much so that, by the end of September, 217,506 had paid to enter, making it the second best season on record. Two new additions to that year's calendar had helped boost attendances and receipts, and would prove to be of particular importance in the Super Swimming Stadium's post-war future.

One was the regular appearance of the Aquabats, billed as 'Britain's Foremost Diving Team'. Their highly professional members performed thrilling acrobatic diving displays laced with stunts and comedy sketches which delighted packed audiences. Over the next few years these would be developed into a longer show featuring synchronised swimmers, music and dancers, eventually evolving into a daily water pageant.

The other, more significant, event took place on July 18th when fourteen young ladies in swimming costumes paraded around the stadium in the first heat of a new competition to find the country's National Bathing Beauty Queen. It was a low-key beginning of what would in time become the celebrated Miss Great Britain Contest and put Morecambe firmly on the map.

RAILWAY POSTERS

During the second half of the 19th century railways played a key role in the establishment and growth of seaside resorts such as Morecambe. In turn, holidaymakers became an important source of revenue for the railway companies. To help publicise the resorts (and to increase passenger numbers) the companies, often in collaboration with local councils, began to produce posters advertising the attractions of holiday destinations in the regions they served.

The first posters tended to be rather dull and uninspiring, usually overloaded with information. They typically comprised a collage of views, often with poor, indecipherable lettering and by no stretch of the imagination could they have been described as 'eye-catching'. However, by the First World War their quality had improved markedly in both image and content. Aided by developments in colour lithography, the railway poster evolved into an effective and relatively cheap form of advertising. The clutter of early examples was replaced by simplicity and clarity – a dominant picture and a reduced text, often little more than the name of the resort and that of the railway company.

Each of the 'Big Four' railway companies created in 1923 – LMS, LNER, GWR and Southern Railway – realised the commercial importance of colourful and informative posters and commissioned specialist graphic designers as well as established artists to produce them. The 1920s and 1930s witnessed the 'golden age' of the poster, a period in which it developed as a distinct art form, characterised by designs of high quality and great visual appeal.

Frank Sherwin (1896-1986) was born in Derby and studied at Derby School of Art and Heatherley's Art School in London. Although a gifted watercolour artist, most of his working life was spent designing posters, particularly for the four main railway companies. In an article for *The Artist* magazine he described his approach to a commission.

"I often deliberately sketch from as high a level as possible in order to give prominence to, say, a promenade or beach and to reduce the sky to a narrow strip. This gives more scope in making interesting groups of small figures or boats. Showing the place to its best advantage ... often necessitates taking many liberties, eliminating undesirable features and emphasising others, with an eye to making an attractive poster."

These elements can clearly be seen in his 1936 poster illustrating Morecambe and Heysham's 'New Luxury Swimming Pool', especially his penchant for artistic licence. The principal figure in the foreground is portrayed sunbathing under a parasol. Her high vantage point overlooking the pool suggests that she is sitting at the edge of the roof of the Midland Hotel – in reality a physical impossibility given the distance between the two buildings. The overall image is stylised, using the bright, flat colouration typical of railway posters of the 1930s, while being representational in its depiction of Morecambe's coastline.

After leaving grammar school in Wolverhampton, **Claude Buckle** (1905-1973) initially trained as an architect before becoming a freelance artist. His first poster commission came from the Southern Railway in 1932 and marked the beginning of a long and prolific career during which he produced over eighty railway posters covering the length and breadth of the United Kingdom.

In his 1949 poster of Morecambe and Heysham for the recently nationalised British Railways, Buckle, like Frank Sherwin, has also taken a high viewpoint, probably the roof of the Midland Hotel. Using a restricted palette of mainly greens and browns, he has achieved a reasonably faithful depiction of Morecambe's seafront with its swimming stadium and ornamental gardens dominating the foreground. In the design, Marine Road and the promenade form two sides of a triangle which meet at a point in the middle distance level with the Central Pier. Here accuracy disappears, the Lakeland Hills in the background having been dramatically foreshortened in order to give a better balance to the overall composition.

FIVE

In the three seasons following the end of World War Two additional entertainment for spectators at the Super Swimming Stadium was largely provided by a succession of exhibition diving teams such as the Aquabats, the Five Anzios, the Javelins and the Trio Salto. One pairing which made regular appearances during this period was that of Leon Marco and Ambrose Smith. Since enthralling the crowd at the first heat of the National Bathing Beauty Contest in July 1945 with their 'Spectacular Diving Display' they had been frequent and popular performers at the stadium.

After the war Leon Marco had visited the United States and been captivated by the Aqua Shows produced by impresario Billy Rose in New York. These were elaborately staged musical and water extravaganzas with hundreds of swimmers, divers, dancers and acrobats all performing to an orchestral accompaniment. Stars of the shows were celebrity swimmers such as Johnny Weismuller, Buster Crabbe, Eleanor Holm and Esther Williams. Inspired by what he saw, Marco wondered if such a show, on a smaller scale, might work in Morecambe and in 1948 he trialled his idea at the Super Swimming Stadium over four days in July. Entitled Leon Marco's *Aquacade*, the programme featured high and exhibition divers, comedy sketches and a water ballet by nine female swimmers known as the Aqualovelies. General admission was 1/- with reserved seats at the deep end 2/6d. The show was well received by the public and returned for more performances in August and September.

Encouraged by the positive response to his *Aquacade*, Marco envisaged an even more ambitious production for the following year. His proposal was for a larger and permanent show with performances every day for the entire season, thus relieving Morecambe Corporation of the need to arrange different attractions each week and potentially providing a regular and relatively stable income. Chairman of the Baths Committee, Councillor James Yates, saw the advantage of such an arrangement, contending that: "Bathers alone, whilst their presence is very welcome, would not keep the baths from being a losing concern."

After a winter of planning, *The Great Water Spectacle of 1949* opened for the season on Sunday 5th June in front of 2,000 spectators. Reporting on the event, which cost nearly £6,000 to put on, the *Visitor* said it had all the glamour, drama and comedy of a stage show presented in the water. 'Star of the show is 20-year old Mildred Netzell, Swedish diving champion since 1944. Her running, one-and-a-half somersault is one of the most thrilling dives in the display. From Denmark have travelled two of that country's ace swimmers, Grethe Hansen and Lis Larsen. They swim with the speed and grace of two sleek young seals. Daring divers Ray Rodgers, Roy True, Johnny Bowers and Jimmy Munlack combine devilment and comedy in the Aquagoons, showing how not to dive! Clever as well as charming are the sixteen Aqualovelies who appear in delightful water ballets. Striking in their red swimsuits the girls combine exceptional talent, grace and precision in their numbers. The fascinating finale of the 1½ hour's show is the wedding of the South Sea Island princess. Towed round the pool in a brightly painted canoe she wears a 20ft waterproof train which is carried by the Aqualovelies. Responsible for the colourful floating effects and costumes is Erik, the well-known London theatrical designer.' *The Great Water Spectacle* ran all summer with performances twice daily at 10.30am and 3.00pm, except Saturdays. Sunday shows were at 3.00pm and 7.00pm, while on Wednesday afternoons there was a performance prior to the Bathing Beauty competition. On certain occasions night owls could enjoy a special 'Moonlight Matinee' beginning at 10.15pm. Admission cost 1/6d or 2/- for a seat.

For the next year's production Leon Marco retained most of the divers – adding Canadian champion Jackie Martin and Betty Slade, eight years European champion, to the team – but decided to cast his net wider for a new set of Aqualovelies. From 400 applicants he selected eighteen girls including local swimmer Elsie Robinson, the only one of the 1949 Aqualovelies to return. Of the other seventeen chosen, thirteen came from London many of whom had only swum as a hobby before joining the show. Unfortunately for the cast, rehearsals were hampered by heavy rain and bitterly cold winds. Despite disruption to its preparations, *The Great Water Spectacle of 1950* opened to acclaim on Whit Sunday and was, in the *Visitor*'s opinion, 'another example of Leon Marco's brilliant amphibious flair'.

In 1951 Leon Marco took his amphibious flair to Bournemouth and the water show at the Super Swimming Stadium had new producers – Roy Fransen and George Baines – and a new cast of divers and swimmers. The first performance of their *Aqua-Revue* was a special free show for Morecambe's hoteliers, boarding house proprietors, shopkeepers, etc. Although this was essentially a promotional exercise, with the audience taking away posters and leaflets to display in their premises, it proved so effective that the event became a traditional fixture at the beginning of each season. George Baines compered the show, the highlight of which was the Swan Lake ballet starring aqua-ballerina Wendy Kirkham, accompanied by the Aquabelles (no longer the Aqualovelies) whose heads and shoulders were encased in hollow casts of model swans. Serious diving was done by the Aquabats and clowning by the Aquamaniacs. In one routine, known as the Monte Cristo escape, a diver was tied in a sack and thrown from the ten metre board, staying underwater for almost a minute before freeing himself and swimming to the surface.

Fransen and Baines brought their *Aqua-Revue* back to Morecambe in 1952 but split up at the end of the season and were replaced in 1953 by producers Jack Payne and Will Hammer. Perhaps trying too hard to outdo previous shows – in title as well as content – their *Gigantic Water Spectacle* was more a succession of variety acts than a typical water show, the divers and swimmers competing for attention with dancers, acrobats,

The Great Water Spectacle of 1949

PROGRAMME

PRODUCTION—LEON MARCO
BALLET MISTRESS—NORAH YOUNG   COMMERE—STELLA MARCO

1. The Mermaid's Ballet of the Flowers
2. All That is New in Swimming .... The Sixteen Aqualovelies
3. Racing the Champ. .... Ray Rogers
4. Sleepy Lagoon .... Johnny Curtis and Ray Rogers
5. Introducing .... The Sixteen Aqualovelies
   Malta's Champion Diver,
   Johnny Bowers
   with 'Professor' Jimmy Munlack
6. Rhythm in the Ballet .... The Sixteen Aqualovelies
7. SHE FLIES THROUGH THE AIR
   featuring MILDRED NETZELL
   Swedish Champion 1944 to 1948
8. Speed ... a 60 metre race presenting Doris Holiday, Yorkshire Champion,
   Lis Larsen of Denmark and Sarah Dyet of Scotland.
9. WALTZ TIME. An Aquaromance .... Norah Young and Ray Rogers
10. Sea Serpent .... The Aqualovelies

—Interval—

11. The Princess of the Islands ROXY
    and The Aqualovelies
12. Hold on to your Hats for . . .
    THE AQUAGOONS
    and to show the difference
    MILDRED NETZELL
13. The Tropical Island Wedding .... a South Sea Island Romance
    The Bride .... Roxy
    The Bridegroom .... Johnny Bowers
    The Bridesmaids .... The Aqualovelies
14. Finale .... On the Island .... Full Company
    THE AQUALOVELIES

Eve Baker   Helen Davies   Sarah Dyet   Nora Young   Ricky O'Hara
Freda Hancox   Grethe Hansen   Doris Holiday   Audrey Firth   Vicky Venus
Jean Jesson   Marie Roche   Lis Larsen   Maureen Howell   Elsie Robinson
Dorothy Pilling   Joan Yeates   Priscilla Stogdon

Programme for the first Aqua Show at Morecambe's Super Swimming Stadium.

Publicity photograph of Swedish diving champion Mildred Netzell which she gave to Roy True in 1949. On the reverse she wrote: "Many thanks for a good season at Morecambe. All the best to Roy. Mildred."

George Baines' wife Vera looked after the accounts for his *Aqua-Revue*. This wage sheet for a week in the 1951 season at Morecambe shows her husband to be the highest paid, followed by the organist Reg Liversedge and Les Jameson, the principal diver who also doubled as 'Aqua-comedian'. The male divers were generally better rewarded than the female swimmers with the exception of Wendy Kirkham, speciality swimmer and choreographer for the Aquabelles.

wire-walkers and stuntmen. Although attendances were reasonably good, Payne and Hammer were not invited back and 1954 saw the return of Leon Marco to the Super Swimming Stadium.

Since leaving Morecambe he had staged similar productions at Bournemouth's Pier Approach Baths and would continue to do so throughout the 1950s and 1960s. Advertised in block capitals as A SPARKLING SHOW IN A SPARKLING POOL, Leon Marco's *Water Show* promised spectators THRILLS! SPILLS!! and SPLASHES!!! However, as Marco was still involved with staging his *Aquafantasia* in Bournemouth, much of the organisation for the Morecambe show was delegated to Jackie Martin who, with fellow diver Swede Gibson, had worked for Marco the previous year. Other ex-Bournemouth performers appearing at Morecambe in 1954 were the aqua-ballerina Dorita (Doreen Watson) and swimmers Joyce Ewen and June Langford. Aspiring participants had to pass rigorous auditions to gain a place in the show. As Jackie Martin explained: "I could advertise for divers and would perhaps receive fifty replies from good divers, but after auditions only three or four would be found suitable." Those making the cut that year included local divers Pete Aspinall and Ray Carter and swimmers Ella Waldie, Elizabeth Western and June Wray.

Opposite: Spectators crane their necks to watch as five interlocked divers fly through the air from the ten metre board.

ROY TRUE, PETE ASPINALL & PERRY BLAKE (Divers)

Roy True came to Morecambe in 1949 with three other divers to take part in an Aqua Show at the Super Swimming Stadium.

"Johnny Bowers, Jimmy Munlack, Johnny Curtis and me were all from the same part of London but had been picked up separately by the show's producer Leon Marco who used to go round the swimming galas looking for divers and swimmers. At the time I was working as an apprentice book-binder, which I didn't much like, so when I was offered a job diving I took it. The money was better too – I think the very first pay I got was £10 a week, and in the second year it went up to £15, doing two shows a day, six days a week. When we got to the stadium Leon Marco said to us: 'Up on the boards lads and I want three dives from you – do whatever you like.' This came as a bit of a shock as none of us had ever seen a ten metre diving board before!

We were all in *The Great Water Spectacle of 1949* which was produced by Leon Marco and compered by his wife. As well as straight diving we also did comedy routines, as the Aquagoons, each lasting about fifteen minutes. One was called the Builders' Act. Four of us would be dressed as builders and were told by a foreman in a bowler hat that there was a problem on the top diving board. He said there was a plank sticking out which needed sawing off. One of us would walk out with a saw and sit on the end of the plank and 'saw' through it. The plank was hinged and only held by wooden pegs so once the pegs were cut the hinges would drop and you would fall off into the water.

In a variation on this, a diver dressed as a workman would be wearing a belt with the back soaked in petrol. He was smoking a cigarette and 'accidentally' set fire to himself and started running around the board before jumping into the water to put the flames out. Yelling to his mates that he couldn't swim they tossed down a bucket on a rope to save him. As they started to pull him up the foreman told one of the men to go and do another job. But the remaining two found the man on the bucket was too heavy for the two who were left and they both got pulled into the pool.

In the winter months after the 1950 season some of us toured the country with a scaled down version of the show which we put on at various Empire Theatres, using a transportable pool. When not performing I did other work, including a job in a car factory which was very well paid but I preferred to do the diving, even though the pay was a bit less. After leaving Morecambe I did similar shows in Blackpool and other resorts – Scarborough, Rhyl, Weston-Super-Mare, Minehead, Bournemouth – and three months in an Aqua Show in Holland as part of a circus. Eventually, I came back to Morecambe to work at Pontins doing three shows a weekend at their holiday camps in Heysham, Blackpool and Southport."

Jimmy Munlack, Johnny Bowers, Roxy Baker and Roy True outside an Empire Theatre during their winter tour of Britain in 1950.

Pete Aspinall joined the water show at the Super Swimming Stadium in 1951. His son, with the same name, remembers as a young boy going to watch his father perform.

"They were summer seasons I will never forget. Mum used to take us three boys and my sister quite regularly, but not as often as I would have liked – I would have gone to every performance if I could and the weather never put us off from attending the shows.

The Aqualoonies were first to do their diving tricks and comedy acts. There was a rather dangerous routine involving a chase around the sun terrace which was a sight to be seen. One of the Aqualoonies was dressed in a gorilla suit and pursued by a hunter in khaki shirt and shorts and a large pith helmet. Armed with a blunderbuss he chased the gorilla around the entire circuit of the terrace. Shots were heard and the gorilla was seen jumping in the air holding his backside as if he had been hit. For its final escape the gorilla leapt off the corner of the terrace to hit the water next to the diving boards, quite a daring stunt. Various other silly dives were performed off the top board including one diver who rode around the platform on a two-wheeled scooter and then went over the end as if by accident, doing a somersault or two before hitting the water.

After the antics of the Aqualoonies the divers got serious and changed out of their silly costumes to perform a series of excellent dives, singly and in unison, to enthral the spectators. Then the Aqualovelies entered the pool to do their synchronised swimming displays. I think the shows lasted about two hours though time seemed to stand still as we watched in amazement.

In the winter months my father was a lorry driver for a Heysham transport firm and supplemented his income by singing in local pubs and clubs under the stage name of Peter Dino, so called because his voice was similar to that of Dean Martin."

In the 1950s the divers at the Super Swimming Stadium were regarded as celebrities, especially by young teenagers of the time. Some, like Pete Aspinall, produced signed photographs to give to their fans.

'Like a swallow in flight the dare-devil diver plunges from the top of the ladder to cleave the water 75 feet below.'

The 'swallow' in the *Visitor* reporter's description was ex-RAF diving champion **Perry Blake** who performed his spectacular feat twice daily during the *Aqua-Revue* at the Super Swimming Stadium in 1952. The steel ladder and tiny platform had recently been purchased from Pinewood Studios where they had been used in the 1951 film *Encore*. Roy Fransen was originally meant to do the tower dive at the stadium but unfortunately had ended up in hospital after an accident. Following the news, producer George Baines assembled all the divers and asked: "Does anyone want to dive off the tower and how much money would you want?" Nobody was keen but eventually Perry Blake said he would do it and, to the astonishment of the other divers, didn't want any extra payment.

By the end of the season Perry's daring exploits had earned him celebrity status. The following spring many people were shocked to hear the news that he had died after a diving mishap. It was therefore something of a surprise to the staff of the *Visitor* when Perry walked into their office at the end of June. An astonished reporter told him: "You're supposed to be dead. Everybody thinks you were killed in a diving accident in Paris some months ago." Perry replied: "I don't know how that rumour got around. I haven't been to Paris. I've been in Edinburgh all winter. My father had a letter from my former landlady in Morecambe asking if I was dead. When I went into a local dance hall at home all my friends looked at me in amazement, they thought I was dead too." He added "I may be dead before the summer is out though – I'm diving 52 feet into nine feet of water at Southport in the show there."

Interviewed six years later in Great Yarmouth where he had joined George Baines' *Water Follies*, Perry recalled the apprehension he felt before his first tower dive at the Super Swimming Stadium. "I was terrified just looking up at it but thought to myself I've got to have a go. Next morning I got up early and with nobody about I went into the pool, climbed up and dived. It was quite a good dive too. Now I try to make every dive perfect – it's not just a matter of hurling myself from a great height like some other high divers." Asked what would happen if he made a mistake, Perry admitted: "I'd rather not think about it. But my insurance is pretty heavy!" His insurance company nearly had to pay out in 1962. In his first practice session of the season, diving from 75 feet into water half the depth of that of Morecambe's pool, Perry struck his head on the bottom. He was hauled out unconscious by fellow performers and rushed to hospital where, to everyone's relief, he made a rapid recovery and was discharged in time for the opening of the show three days later.

After leaving Morecambe Perry became an enthusiastic body-builder. By 1959 he had bulked up to a muscular seventeen stone and was billed as 'Europe's heaviest and most graceful high diver' in his first season at Great Yarmouth. Perry is seen here at the resort's pool with a somewhat slimmer Roy Walsh who represented Great Britain at the Melbourne Olympic Games in 1956. Roy later moved to Morecambe and appeared in several shows at the Super Swimming Stadium in the mid-1960s.

Contemplating the diversity of the show's cast, the *Visitor* wondered in how many places one would find working together 'a man who used to wrestle an alligator, an artist who spends his winter tucked away in a Paris studio, a crack Danish gymnast, a salesman and a chef, a girl whose ambition it is to keep an orphanage, a Morecambe bathing beauty housewife, a girl who loves opera, a telephonist, a waitress, and many other young people with varied experience'. As for the show itself … 'Its star is Danish international gymnast Knud Hakonson who gave an exhibition of his abilities on the high bar erected on the stage in front of the fountain. Also from Denmark was Tova Bach, a ladies swimming champion who had a solo spot in the show. Outstanding in the diving team were Jackie Martin and Swede Gibson, who thrilled the audience with their spectacular jockey dive. There was good support from Don Morris and Pete Aspinall. The Aquabelles delighted with their rhythmic swimming, and the crazy antics of the Aquagoons on the diving tower greatly amused.'

Having noted the growing popularity of the stadium's water shows since their inception, Morecambe Corporation decided to dispense with outside promoters for the 1955 season and organise the event itself. In previous years a type of franchise arrangement had been in place with producers such as Leon Marco, Roy Fransen and George Baines devising each show and paying the divers, swimmers, organist and other staff, with Morecambe Corporation receiving an agreed proportion of the receipts. By bringing production 'in house' the Corporation was confident it could increase its share of the overall income generated.

Baths Superintendent George Campbell Cooper was given responsibility for that year's show. Since his appointment in 1950 he had worked closely with the various producers and had acquired, he believed, sufficient expertise to stage his own interpretation. In the event his *Aqua-Cascades* kept to the well-tried format of specialist divers and swimmers, themed set-pieces with the (reinstated) Aqualovelies and comedy routines from the (newly christened) Aqualoonies. The show set the template for the next decade until the untimely death of Campbell Cooper in 1965. One often overlooked outcome of the continuity provided by Morecambe Corporation was that it enabled Campbell Cooper to develop a company of tried and trusted performers, with certain individuals staying for several years, in contrast to the large turnover which characterised the earlier external productions.

The 1955 *Aqua-Cascades* opened on Sunday 29th May but soon ran into trouble. That summer, Morecambe was being visited by activists of the Lord's Day Observation Society who were touring the town to ensure that businesses complied with the requirements of the Sunday Entertainments Act of 1932. The Corporation, worried that some aspects of its show at the Super Swimming Stadium might infringe the Act's provisions, requested modifications to the Sunday programme. There was to be no comedy diving (was laughter not permitted on the Sabbath?) and the girl dancers could not perform (presumably bare arms and legs were only acceptable if their owners were half submerged in the water). Normal service was resumed during the rest of the week but the restrictions eventually led to the abandonment of Sunday performances.

1. OVERTURE - - - Arthur Gaisford
2. SWIM TIME - - The Aquabelles
3. PIRATES - - - Comedy Team
4. EVOLUTION OF SWIMMING Tova
5. THE RACE
6. EXHIBITION OF GYMNASTICS
   Knud Hakonson
7. SOLO SWIM - - Aquaballerina
8. WATER MOSAIC - - Aquabelles
9. THEY FLY THROUGH THE AIR
   Diving
10. HIGHLAND AQUACADE Aquabelles
11. SECOND HALF OVERTURE
12. SOPHISTICATED LADIES
    The Aquabelles
13. CHAMP v. THE CHUMP
14. A SWIMMING DUO
    Tova and Don Morris
15. CUBAN RHYTHM - The Aquabelles
16. THE PSYCHIATRIST'S DELIGHT
    The Aquagoons
17. WEDDING IN THE SOUTH SEAS
18. FINALE

The programme for Leon Marco's *Water Show* of 1954 gives an indication of the variety of entertainment provided.

The 'South Sea Island' themed set-piece was a perennial favourite with the public, offering 'grass skirts, wonderful figures, sunburn, golden sand and lilting music'.

As well as exhibition diving and swimming, the stadium's Aqua Shows included a number of comedy routines performed by a group of divers who, over the years, were known by various names – Aquagoons, Aquamaniacs, Aquazaniacs – before finally settling on Aqualoonies.

Striped costumes were favoured in the early days with antics mainly restricted to the diving boards.

Later the routines became more involved …

… with some based at the poolside …

… and others utilising the terraces and walls of the stadium.

Divers Swede Gibson and Don Morris prepare to throw a young Charlie Overett from the ten metre board. As a boy, Charlie went with his friends to the swimming pool so often that he got to know the Aqualoonies well and was invited to join one of their routines.

"These guys were like heroes to me, an eleven-year old. They were celebrities and really nice people. I became part of the act on the weekend and on Wednesday afternoon when I wasn't at school. They got me to sit on the end of the diving board and would 'hit' me with a plank and I'd roll off the end into a dive. The first time I was a little nervous but soon gained confidence. When the act finished I'd go back up and join them on the board and they would hold my hand up … and chuck me in again!"

Dancers, gymnasts and other non-water based acts became regular features of Campbell Cooper's productions, including Babu Rao, 'India's Wonder of the Slack Wire', in 1956, acrobatic dancers The Three Jays in 1957 and, topping the bill in 1958, The Nimros, famous trick and comedy cyclists. In Campbell Cooper's opinion the 1958 *Aqua-Cascades*, with its mixture of diving, swimming, dancing, acrobatics and comedy, was the complete family show and contained "something for everybody". However, everybody did not include members of Morecambe Corporation's Finance Committee who were unhappy with the level of income being generated by the water show and questioned the desirability of continuing to sponsor it. "Has the time arrived", asked Alderman Parks, "when the Swimming Stadium should be used for swimming only, and the Baths Superintendent better employed looking after the baths?" Chairman of the Baths Committee, Councillor Ernest Kershaw (who had replaced James Yates) vigorously rejected the suggestion, claiming there was nothing wrong with the show. "The high diving is thrilling and expertly performed. The comedy work is good, and I do not see how anyone can fail to be amused. The girls do all that can be expected of them, and many people like to see that kind of swimming." His view was backed up by the Vice-chairman, Councillor Frank Higginson, who claimed: "This is an amenity we cannot do without. People get wonderful value for money with this show along with their admission to the baths." The *Visitor* added its support, contending that there could be little doubt that many people were attracted to the stadium who would not go there but for the show. While conceding that recent receipts had been disappointing, Campbell

Cooper pointed out that attendances were very much weather dependent and that the previous two summers had been unseasonably cool and wet. His assessment gained credence the following year when, thanks to a warmer and drier summer coupled with a show described by the *Visitor* as 'the best of the lot', profits almost trebled.

The *Aqua-Cascades* was an expensive show to stage. Campbell Cooper insisted on the best quality outfits, usually obtained from London suppliers. His productions typically included three or four set-pieces based on places around the world, each requiring the appropriate costumes and background effects. The divers, swimmers and dancers were well remunerated as were the speciality acts topping the bill. While expenditure on the show changed little over the years, income tended to fluctuate wildly. Unfortunately, as most of the financial outlay occurred at the start of a season and receipts were at the mercy of the vagaries of the weather, predicting whether or not the show would return a profit was something of a lottery.

In 1955 Campbell Cooper's inaugural show coincided with a glorious summer and made a surplus of £3,221. The following year poor weather saw this figure drop dramatically to £202 before recovering to £506 in 1957. This see-saw pattern continued until 1961 when, for the first time, the *Aqua-Cascades* recorded a loss (of £152), the result of a very wet summer. Early season downpours did not augur well for the 1962 edition of the show but the *Visitor* attempted to strike a positive note with an encouraging review. 'After a number of postponements through inclement weather, the *Aqua-Cascades* is now well on its way to being one of the Lancashire resort's most popular shows. Originality always seems to be the keynote of Mr G. Campbell Cooper's productions and he contrives to incorporate some effective scenes into this show, such as "Sleepy Lagoon" and "South Seas". In the closing "Cleopatra" item the effect is heightened by the use of a cascading waterfall on the centre stage. The first-class acrobatic and adagio dancing speciality of Erik and Juel tops the bill and there is an excellent diving act from the talented team of Don Morris, Ed Lashbrook, Eric and Eve, Bill Paterson and film stunt man Ray Carter. Dorothy Carty is aqua-choreographer and aqua-ballerina and has the Aqualovelies with her in a number of swimming specialities. The vocal numbers this year are provided by June Wray, a singer who creates exactly the right atmosphere for a show of this kind, and dancing specialities, devised by Carol Michele, are put over by the Gay Steppers. Comedy in the pool and on the diving boards comes from Vic Ward and Peter Hellewell with assistance from the various members of the diving team. Don Morris, Ray Carter and Peter Hellewell also combine in a trampoline number.'

The show, however, was dogged by bad weather throughout the summer. Audiences did pick up towards the end of the season but not in sufficient numbers to prevent another loss, this time the much larger figure of £862. Concerned that the future of the *Aqua-Cascades* might be under threat Campbell Cooper wondered if the Baths Committee might prefer a smaller show, perhaps dispensing with the dancers and/ or cutting back on the stage sets. The Committee reassured him that it wanted the existing format of the show to be retained. It was reluctant to compromise on the high production values that the public had come to expect and was optimistic that, if the weather was kinder over the next couple of seasons, the expected increase in receipts would balance out the recent deficits.

In front of the stadium's main entrance passers-by were vociferously encouraged to "Come on in – see A Sparkling Show in a Sparkling Pool".

Opposite: A circle of synchronised perfection by sixteen Aqualovelies.

Babu Rao, 'India's Wonder on the Slack Wire'.

The Three Jays, acrobatic dancers.

LOUIE CARRICK (Aqualovely)

Louie Carrick was offered the chance to be an Aqualovely when aged sixteen but her parents objected and she had to wait until she was 21 and had left home before joining the *Aqua-Cascades*.

"The producer of the shows was Campbell Cooper and we started rehearsals in early May. We did two weeks rehearsing and often it was freezing. In fact, on one occasion there was a thin layer of ice on the water – and that was salt water so it was very cold! The shows started in late May and finished the first week in September. Each one began with an organist and lasted about two hours. We did a show in the morning and another in the afternoon, with an evening performance on Sunday. We had Saturdays off. The pay wasn't bad – the first wage I got was £9 a week which was more than I was earning working in a shop. Each year after Christmas Campbell Cooper asked me to model the bathing suits for the new season and he'd then pick the ones he liked best. We always had top quality costumes because they had to be hard-wearing to last the season.

In the show there were divers who also did clowning about as the Aqualoonies but they were actually like gymnasts and some had been to the Olympics. There were dancers called the Gay Steppers who didn't swim. We also had a singer, escapologist, magician, trick cyclists, and even a wire-walker. Every year the show had different themes – South Seas, Egyptian, Greek, Spanish, Dutch and so on. We dressed up in costume and usually did a bit of dancing before going in the water. The routines were worked out by our choreographer Dorothy Carty and we mainly did synchronised swimming with leg kicks, forward pikes and back somersaults and making patterns in the water like stars and circles. Each piece tended to last between ten and twelve minutes. Sometimes we had packed audiences on a lovely day. Other times there would be just a few people under the café sheltering from the rain. We still had to do a show even if there were only six in.

The divers were like family and had respect for us. There was no hanky-panky but they were always playing tricks on us. One day we had finished the show and went to get changed but couldn't find our underwear anywhere. Then we saw that strung out from the flagpole was a line of bras and knickers blowing in the breeze! But it was all good fun and we got on really well.

We met lots of stars on the Miss Great Britain days as we did two spots before and after the beauty competition. Whoever was top of the bill at the Winter Gardens came to judge the contestants. I remember once when we were dressed as leopards and had to run through the gents' changing room to get to where we had to start, and coming towards us was our producer with Adam Faith.

Louie Carrick as Cleopatra in 1962.

The full cast of 'Cleopatra', finale of the *Aqua-Cascades* in 1962.

Back row (left to right): Joyce Southern, Jennifer Elwood, Beverley Richards, Ed Lashbrook, Ray Carter, Don Morris, Bill Paterson, Pete Hellewell and June Wray.

Middle row: Zoe Edmondson, Irene Shaw, Barbara Leigh, Louie Carrick, Carol Carter, Ann Earnshaw and Valerie Settle.

Front row: Christine Anyon and Nadine Ellison

He was very handsome but only as tall as me. He shook hands with us and then we had to hurry to begin our act. On another occasion we were on the stage with David Whitfield and Hughie Green. Something must have been said as David pushed Hughie into the water. We all laughed but he was very angry and threatened to sue. Nobody liked Hughie Green.

I stayed at the Super Swimming Stadium until 1966 and then did other shows in places like Blackpool and Southport until I was 42. The *Aqua-Cascades* was a very good show and it was a shame when it finished. People said it was glamorous but it wasn't glamorous, it was hard work. But I was very happy – it was a way of life."

JUNE WRAY (Vocalist)

June Wray holds the unique distinction of reaching the Grand Final of the National Bathing Beauty Contest three times and also having three spells as a performer in the Aqua Shows at the Super Swimming Stadium. However, her ambition after leaving school was to be on the stage. She was a talented singer and won acclaim as the lead female role in the musical *Hit the Deck* at Morecambe Winter Gardens theatre when only seventeen. Other shows followed as did her first appearance in the final of the NBBC in 1949. Unlike many contestants June could also swim and was invited by Leon Marco to join his *Great Water Spectacle* at the swimming stadium.

"I came as a replacement at the end of 1950 and did the whole of the 1951 season. The choreographer for the show was Wendy Kirkham who helped me improve my swimming by getting me to do lengths of the pool using my legs only. Wendy was the star of the Swan Lake ballet we did that year. She was dressed in a beautiful white costume while the rest of us had our heads and shoulders hidden in hollow papier-mâché casts of model swans. We circled round her, treading water and hardly able to see. It was horrible, very claustrophobic. The ballet finished with Wendy doing her 'dying swan' bit and we silently kept urging her to 'die! die!' so we could get the swans off our heads and breathe properly.

When the season finished George Baines, the producer – a lovely man – offered me a job in a show he was putting on in Bournemouth but I had just got

The 1951 Aquabelles with June Wray (back row, fourth from right). Star swimmer and choreographer Wendy Kirkham stands out in her white costume.

June Wray at the Super Swimming Stadium in 1962.

married and wanted to start a family. I left the show but returned in 1954, a year in which it never seemed to stop raining. One of the divers who helped me a lot at this time was Don Morris who was also a very good swimmer. We developed this act called *The Lonely Ballerina* in which I dived into the pool and swam round on my own pretending to be lonely and forlorn. Don was on the top board and I'd see him and wave and he'd dive in. I'd do a back somersault underneath the water and we'd both come to the surface and swim together. It was done to nice music and people said it was a lovely routine.

I also used to sing from the café balcony before the beauty competitions on a Wednesday afternoon, usually a medley of songs from the shows. On one occasion Julie Andrews, who was appearing at the Winter Gardens that week, was helping to judge a heat. I had been singing *Sleepy Lagoon* when one of the attendants came dashing up to me and said 'Julie Andrews says you've got a lovely voice'. Praise indeed! In the evenings I would sing in the Parisian Bar at the Winter Gardens and do musical shows and pantomimes in the winter months.

After another break I came back for the last time in 1962, mainly as a vocalist, and became more involved with helping Campbell Cooper devise the themes for his *Aqua-Cascades* and choose the songs. We always used to have a Hawaiian set, with grass skirts and wiggling hips, and me singing things like *Song of the Islands* and *Pagan Love Song*. For a French theme I would do *Under the Bridges of Paris* and *Moon River* – one of my favourites – and *Tulips from Amsterdam* for a Dutch one. Depending on the weather we also did some evening shows as well. All the pool was floodlit from underneath and it looked really beautiful. The water was kept immaculate and was lovely and clean and clear.

I was much older than the others by this time and had to 'mother' the younger girls, some of whom could be a handful and not always reliable. I always said what we wanted was nice married women with children because they needed the money and would stick at it. I seemed to have a lot of responsibility but no real power so when I became pregnant again in 1965 I decide to call it a day and left, this time for good."

Complimentary ticket for the special free performance of the 1963 *Aqua-Cascades*.

Optimism was soon dented by the coming of 'The Big Freeze'. The winter of 1962/3 was one of the coldest and longest on record in Britain, only releasing its Arctic grip at the beginning of March. Eight-inch thick ice covered the pool in the Super Swimming Stadium and had to be broken up by workmen with pick-axes and crowbars so that the basin could be painted for the coming season. Fortunately, preparations managed to be completed in time for the annual free performance of the 1963 *Aqua-Cascades*, which was enjoyed by an audience of 4,000. In one eye-catching scene the Gay Steppers and Aqualovelies danced around a Maypole to traditional tunes before members of the company appeared wearing old-type swimming costumes and then, in a nod to the popular crazes of the time, the cast demonstrated how to dance the Twist, the Jive and the Madison. Especially striking was the show's finale, "Daughters of the Sun", which featured a large Buddhist statue on the stage.

A variety of geographical locations characterised the 1964 show with the company rapidly changing costumes for "Grecian Fantasy", "Roman Holiday", "South Seas" and "Tulip Time", the last performed in front of a mock Dutch windmill. Sadly, Campbell Cooper saw little of that year's production having been taken ill with a suspected heart attack when attending a Baths Committee meeting. After a month in hospital he was able to return home but needed to recuperate for several weeks. In his absence former Police Chief Inspector Edward Pinder took temporary charge. It turned out to be a fortuitous appointment as on the Friday before the August Bank Holiday a gang of some forty teenage 'Rockers' invaded the stadium and ran amok around the pool, frightening parents and their children. Calling on his police experience Pinder, with the assistance of his staff, chased them round to the front entrance before ejecting them onto the promenade. "It was the only way to deal with them", he said. "They could have caused some trouble had I taken no action. Some of them paid to get in but others climbed up a rear drainpipe, clambered over the balcony and gained entrance that way." The Bank Holiday weekend provided a textbook example in microcosm of how attendances at the stadium were affected by the weather. Saturday was wet and miserable; Sunday dull with occasional glimpses of the sun; Monday much brighter with several hours of sunshine. A meagre 84 hardy souls passed through the turnstiles on Saturday, increasing to 674 on Sunday, then more than tripling to 2,327 on Monday.

Campbell Cooper was back in charge for the beginning of the 1965 season and by the end of May rehearsals for the first performance of the *Aqua-Cascades* on Thursday 3rd June were nearly complete. At the dress rehearsal on the preceding Friday he had complained of chest pains and was admitted to Morecambe Hospital the next day. His condition steadily deteriorated and he died on June 2nd the day before his new production was to open. Edward Pinder again took over as acting Baths Superintendent for the remainder of the season until a permanent appointment could be made. He was one of five applicants who were shortlisted and interviewed for the position but lost out to 29-year old Glynn D. Smith, then Deputy Borough Baths Manager at Islington, London.

The cast of 'Tulip Time' from the *Aqua-Cascades* of 1964.

Vocalist June Wray stands under the windmill flanked by (from left to right) dancers The Gay Steppers (Virginia Baum, Janet Coop and Cherie Bell) and Aqualovelies (Kathleen Smith, Anne Earnshaw, June Dyson, Annette Ramsay, Chris Anyon and, seated, Pat Adams, Louie Carrick and Barbara Leigh).

Since the early 1950s excerpts from each year's Aqua Show bookended the programme of the Grand Final of the Miss Great Britain competition.

The show's diving team pose for the camera at the 1965 final. Clockwise from the seated Eve Smith are Bill Paterson, Ron Fyfe, Ed Lashbrook, Eric Smith and Roy Walsh.

The changing graphic styles of programme covers for Campbell Cooper's *Aqua-Cascades*.

Like vultures circling over a dying animal, members of Morecambe Corporation's Finance Committee saw the demise of Campbell Cooper as a timely opportunity to pursue their antipathy towards the water show. Still dismayed about its cost – the 1965 *Aqua-Cascades* had lost £600 – the Committee officially requested that it be discontinued. This was turned down at the January 1966 meeting of the Town Council by nineteen votes to fourteen, mainly on the grounds that the show had already been included in the coming season's Holiday Guide and councillors 'would look fools' if it was not allowed to take place. They had an obligation to visitors and the new Baths Manager (as he was now titled) should be given a chance to do one show before a final decision was made. Morecambe remained the only place in the country where an open-air water show was staged.

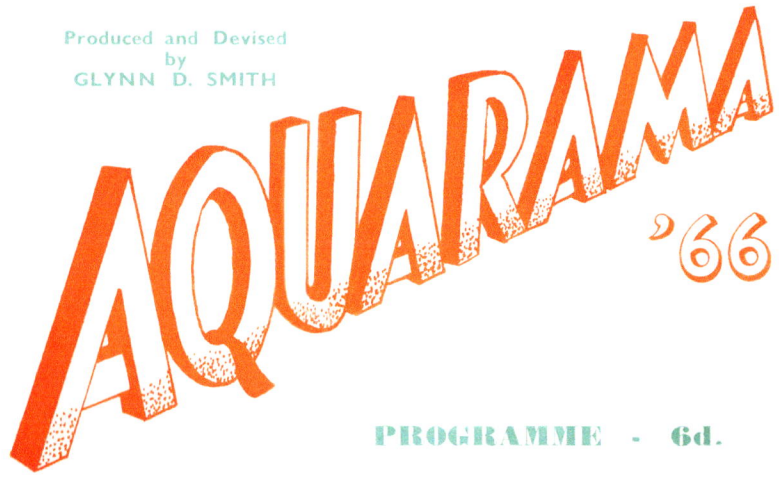

Part of the programme cover for the last Aqua Show at the Super Swimming Stadium.

While realising that his *Aquarama '66* could well be the stadium's last, Glynn Smith nevertheless devised a programme very much in keeping with its predecessors, the professionalism of the experienced performers ensuring that the high standards of previous productions were maintained. Acts included the husband and wife diving partnership Los Delgados (Eric and Eve Smith) and Eddie & Pauline, experts on the slack wire. Although the show had a passable season the writing was on the wall. Rising costs and falling attendances finally persuaded councillors that, after nearly two decades, it was time to wield the axe. There would be no *Aquarama '67*.

In its place Glynn Smith opted for a greater focus on swimming and associated sports. Swimming championships and water polo matches would be held on Saturdays throughout the season and top divers and swimmers would be invited to give demonstrations. Tuesday afternoons would be 'Competition Time' where swimmers and non-swimmers of all ages could compete for prizes in a range of different events. One attraction not affected by the changes was the Miss Great Britain contest which continued to be held on Wednesday afternoons. Smith believed that keeping the stadium as free for as much of the week as possible for swimming and sunbathing was the right approach. "Any special event will only succeed if the weather is good, and if it is good then all the public want to do is relax in the sun and water."

Although the water show in Morecambe was no more, the stadium's diving team did not disband. Under the leadership of Bill Paterson, experienced divers Ray Carter, Ed Lashbrook and Roy Walsh, plus teenage newcomer Trevor Horn, took their exhibition and comedy diving to other venues, including the Pontins holiday camps at Heysham, Blackpool and Southport – even, on occasions, returning to perform at the Super Swimming Stadium. Nonetheless, the Corporation's decision to cancel the show

DON THOMPSON (Organist)

In the first years of Morecambe's Aqua Shows the swimmers performed their routines to recorded music but by the early 1950s records had been replaced by an organist who was responsible for accompanying the various acts as well as having a couple of solo spots. According to vocalist June Wray some were better than others! In her opinion Don Thompson was one of the best.

Born in Kendal, Don Thompson fell in love with the organ after being taken as a child to see Reginald Dixon as Blackpool's Tower Ballroom. By the age of sixteen he was assistant organist at Kentmere church and two years later performed his first concerts at churches in Germany. After graduating from Cambridge University he became well-known as one of the North of England's leading entertainers, appearing in ballrooms and nightclubs all over the region.

Operating from his kiosk under the café he spent five years as resident organist and compere at Morecambe's Super Swimming Stadium between 1957 and 1961 before emigrating to California and embarking on a successful career during which he recorded more than fifty albums of organ music.

Don Thompson in his kiosk beneath the stadium café.

appeared to have ben vindicated when Glynn Smith, in his annual report of 1968, was able to announce that income from swimming alone had never been higher and, without the show, expenditure had been considerably less. To increase revenue he urged the Corporation to consider the installation of sauna baths, pointing out that at other pools they were very popular and made "handsome profits".

In marked contrast, his report two years later was decidedly downbeat. Attendances were the worst since 1962 due to bad weather, his appeal for the provision of sauna baths was still falling on deaf ears and he was becoming increasingly concerned about the physical condition of the stadium. It had not been painted for five years and there had been a noticeable deterioration in its fabric over the previous eighteen months. The concrete terraces were cracking badly and urgently needed attention while many of the 240 wooden benches required repair and would have to be replaced before long.

By 1972 serious structural weaknesses in the building had become apparent and although £6,000 was spent to make the stadium safe to open the following year, a much larger sum would be needed to guarantee its future. The Borough Engineer, Derek Illsley, estimated that an outlay of a further £30,000 could extend the stadium's life for another year or so but having seen the poor state of its foundations he concluded that the building was "beyond economic restoration" and advised its demolition and replacement.

Visitors to the stadium after it opened for the 1973 season could see some of the problems for themselves and the measures that had been taken for their safety. The pool itself had not been affected but the diving boards and large chute could not be used and the area behind had been roped off to prevent access. In addition there had been a certain amount of shoring up in the cordoned off parts and also on the sunbathing terrace near the café.

1974 brought the reorganisation of local government and the merging of Morecambe and Lancaster into one authority. The newly created Lancaster City Council inherited responsibility for the Super Swimming Stadium and with it an unwelcome dilemma – to retain and repair or demolish and replace. Before the issue could be properly debated news came in early May that the planned opening of the swimming pool had been postponed following the discovery of a leak which was causing the loss of around 9,000 gallons of water a day. An emergency meeting of the Council's Economic Development Committee decided that the pool should be emptied to allow examination by specialist contractors. Allan Heppenstall, the Council's Planner/Architect, recommended in the strongest terms that the stadium should not be used by the public until the leak had been investigated. To the disappointment of residents and visitors alike the Super Swimming Stadium remained closed over the Spring Bank Holiday for the first time in its history.

Baths Manager Glynn D. Smith (right) stands next to Geoffrey Thompson, Publicity and Entertainments Manager, and Frank Higginson, Chairman of the Baths Committee.

THE PRODUCERS

Of the eighteen Aqua Shows staged at Morecambe's Super Swimming Stadium between 1949 and 1966, all but two were produced either by Leon Marco, Roy Fransen and George Baines or George Campbell Cooper.

Born in Leicester, **Leon Marco** (Markson) learned to dive at the local swimming pool before joining the Merchant Navy and travelling the world. After World War Two he became a professional exhibition diver and spent time in the United States. While in New York he met ex-Olympic swimmer Johnny Weismuller and persuaded him to come to Britain to star in a show at Blackpool's Derby Baths in 1949. This was the same year that Marco put on his *Great Water Spectacle* at the Super Swimming Stadium, having turned to producing following a serious neck injury which curtailed his diving exploits. Its success led to further shows, not only in Morecambe but at other venues around the country, most notably Bournemouth, a resort with which he had a long association. He was also active in Europe, devising a ten-week series for RAI Television in Italy with producer Mario Minasi for which they won a Silver Rose of Montreux. Returning from the continent he settled in Bournemouth and continued to present water shows in the town until his early death in 1971.

Londoner **Roy Fransen** was already an experienced diver when he met his future partner in the wartime police force. A Yorkshireman from Keighley, **George Baines** had represented the police in diving competitions and was seen as an ideal recruit for a team of divers and stuntmen that Fransen was putting together to tour the country after the war. Joined by three other divers, including ex-beauty queen Vera Beaumont, the Aquabats drove from town to town, towing their own diving tank which they set up at each venue. From small beginnings the act gradually developed into a full scale resident water show (the *Aqua-Revue*), first staged at Bournemouth's Pier Approach Baths in 1948. Described as 'a mix of acrobatic water skills, beauty and comedy', it arguably set the pattern for water shows held at indoor and outdoor pools in Britain during the 1950s.

After bringing their *Aqua-Revue* to Morecambe in 1950 and 1951 Fransen and Baines went their separate ways. Roy Fransen toured with his own version of the show, later paring down its contents to focus on his own pièce-de-résistance – the spectacular 'Dive of Death'. For this he would don a silver-painted cotton boiler suit doused with petrol. Petrol would also be spread across the surface of a relatively shallow tank of water, 16 feet (5 metres) in diameter.

Leon Marco and his wife Stella in 1948. A stylish dresser, Marco was, according to his son, a strong, friendly and generous man, not overtly talkative but one who would command a room when he entered. Something of an adventurer, he competed in the Monte Carlo Rally in 1962 driving the family Jaguar and also won the Attwood trophy for the fastest time around England in the RAC National Rally.

The Aquabats pictured in 1946. Roy Fransen (back centre) was best man at the wedding of George Baines (back right) and Vera Beaumont (front left).

Both would then be set alight and a blazing Fransen would plummet into the fiery water from a height of 75 feet (23 metres). Remarkably, his dangerous and bizarre career lasted until he reached the age of 69 when, during a performance in London in 1985, he misjudged the angle of his dive and died from his injuries.

George Baines trod a somewhat safer path, presenting his *Water Follies* throughout the 1950s at Great Yarmouth. After three seasons at Bournemouth in the early 1960s he moved into the hospitality business in Norfolk, building the Ponderosa Holiday Park in Hopton-on-Sea and then the Broadway Motel in Great Yarmouth, specialising in Country & Western entertainment. In 1976, after having sold his properties, he was asked by Bournemouth Corporation to devise a new Aqua Show. Although the main water-based ingredients remained, it also incorporated circus elements including tightrope walkers, trapeze artistes and animal acts such as performing sea-lions! George Baines died in 1982, his wife and daughter shouldering responsibility for the show until 1984.

Unlike his predecessors, **George Campbell Cooper** had not been a professional diver before producing water shows; his background was in swimming pool management. An urbane and well-spoken Londoner, Campbell Cooper was appointed Baths Superintendent at the Super Swimming Stadium in 1950. Prior to moving to Morecambe he had been manager of Aldershot's open-air pool and the baths at Surbiton. Over the fifteen years of his tenure he presided over what many consider to be the most successful period in the stadium's history.

George Campbell Cooper.

As well as overseeing the day-to-day running of the swimming pool, Campbell Cooper took over the organisation of the water show in 1955 when Morecambe Corporation decided to end its association with outside producers. Conceived to provide all-round family entertainment, his *Aqua-Cascades* proved popular with the public, achieving an eleven year unbroken run. However, as his daughter recalled, it was an all-consuming job. During the season her father worked long hours, seven days a week and was seldom at home. Even in winter there was maintenance and planning to occupy his time although he did manage to spend some weekends with his family. Eventually, the continual stress told and in June 1965 he suffered a fatal heart attack, dying the day before the opening performance of that year's *Aqua-Cascades*.

Campbell Cooper enjoying a swim.

STADIUM SNIPPETS

PREPARING FOR THE SEASON

Maintenance work at the Super Swimming Stadium was continuous throughout the year but the period around Easter was a particularly busy time for stadium staff.

Workmen needed a head for heights when painting the diving tower …

… and putting the finishing touches to the guardrails on the ten metre diving board.

Opposite top: With the pool drained of water, the empty basin could be checked and painted. X marks the spot which divers tried to aim for.

Opposite: Jim Ferguson with the somewhat boring task of refreshing the lines of the swimming lanes.

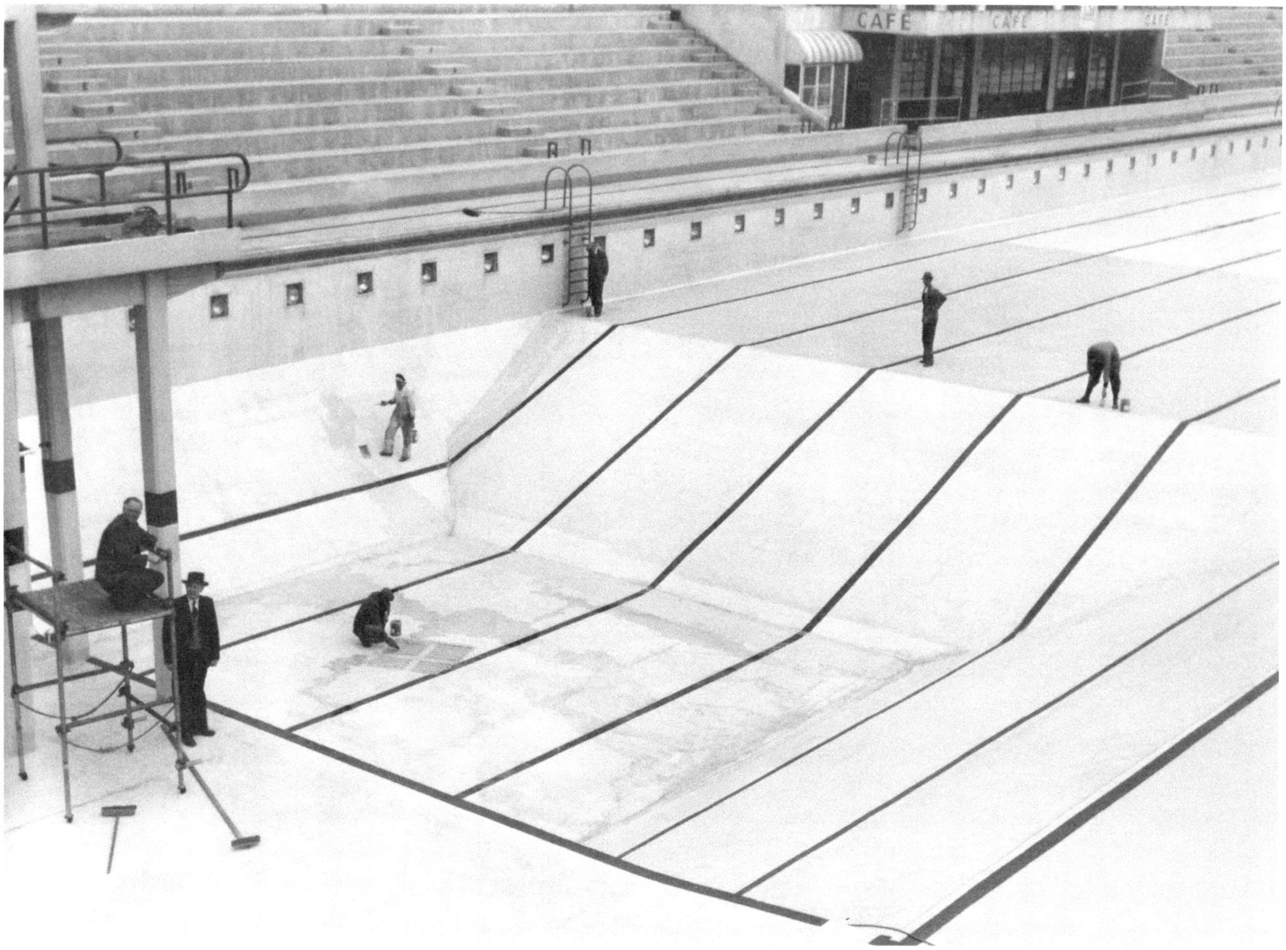

Diving from the Super Swimming Stadium's high board was not for the faint-hearted – it was a long way down to the water! Trevor Horn joined the diving team in the mid-1960s and remembers having to adjust to the outdoor environment.

"Although the top board was the same height as others at covered pools you always seemed higher because there was nothing around you. In winter I would go to the indoor Derby Baths at Blackpool to practise and if you were doing a somersault dive you could see the ceiling and get your bearings but at Morecambe all you could see was sky. And you were also diving into icy cold seawater, so if you got a dive wrong and slapped the water it really hurt."

Diving was a physically demanding occupation and daily performances throughout the season required both strength and stamina. Many divers followed rigorous fitness regimes to build up muscles and endurance, as is illustrated in this photograph of Jack 'Tarzan' Lambert and George 'Swede' Gibson, two divers who appeared in Aqua Shows at the Super Swimming Stadium.

Dancers were an integral part of the *Aqua-Cascades* from the mid-1950s, having their own spots in the shows and also performing with the Aqualovelies – but not joining them in the water! The Gay Steppers first appeared as a dancing trio in 1955 and although the personnel changed over the years the name was retained. In this publicity photograph from 1964 the dancers are (left to right) Virginia Baum, Janet Coop and Cherie Bell.

A trampoline display featured regularly in the *Aqua-Cascades* programme, the performers having names such as The Jumping Crackers, Jumping Jax and The Rebounders. Organist Don Thompson's kiosk can be seen underneath the café.

A focal point in the swimming stadium was the fountain or cascade. Circular in plan and tiered like a wedding cake, it formed the last stage in the cleansing and purification process, aerating the water before it re-entered the pool. An attractive feature in itself, it also rapidly acquired a secondary, though sometimes frowned upon, role as the ideal backdrop for a photo-opportunity. Often the cascade's tumbling water would be totally obscured by bathers cramming the ledges to have their picture taken.

Models from Windsor Water Woollies use the (dry) fountain to show off the latest swimsuits before the opening of the Super Swimming Stadium in July 1936.

NEW STYLE & COLOUR IN SWIM WEAR

Bathing mannequins make a colourful pyramid on the cascade before the water was turned on.—" Visitor " photo.

Smiling bathers have climbed up the fountain for a group picture, turning a blind eye to the notices requesting them not to do so.

'The Fleet's in Port'. Symmetrically arranged on the fountain, Aqualovelies and dancers are photographed for a nautical-themed item included in the programme of the 1963 *Aqua-Cascades*.

BOROUGH OF MORECAMBE & HEYSHAM
(BATHS DEPARTMENT)
DATES TO REMEMBER, 1959
(SEASON TICKET HOLDERS KINDLY NOTE)

May	11th	Opening of Stadium.
May	13th	Local Heat "Miss Great Britain" National Bathing Beauty Contest.
—19th Aug.		Weekly Heats "Miss Great Britain" National Bathing Beauty Contest, organised entirely by Morecambe and Heysham Corporation.
May	31st	First of Special "Sunday Programmes" of Swimming and Diving, and each Sunday throughout the Season, until Sunday, 30th August, 1959.
June	1st	Opening Show "Aqua-Cascades 1959" at 2.45 p.m.
June	4th	Invitation Show "Aqua-Cascades 1959" at 7.0 p.m. (Hotels and Boarding Housekeepers).
June	13th	Sea Cadet Gala — Northern Area.
June	27th	Inter-Schools Gala.
July	4th	Morecambe and Heysham A.S.C.
July	11th	England v. Wales International Water Polo.
July	18th	N.C.A.S.A. Championships Men's 220 yds. Freestyle. Junior Ladies' 220 yds. Freestyle. Ladies' High Diving.
July	25th	St. John Ambulance and Nursing Cadet Swimming Gala.
Aug.	26th	Grand Final "Miss Great Britain" National Bathing Beauty Contest.
Sept.	2nd	"Miss Morecambe" Contest.

(SATURDAYS 1.0 to 5.0 p.m.)

"Aqua-Cascades 1959" presented by Morecambe and Heysham Corporation.

Produced and devised by Campbell Cooper.

Performed twice daily (except all day Saturday and Wednesday mornings) at 10.45 a.m. and 2.45 p.m.

PRICES: Adults 2/3d. and 1/9d.   Juniors 1/3d.

SPECIAL "SUNDAY PROGRAMMES" of Swimming and Diving at 2.45 p.m. and 7.0 p.m.

All the Season—Blue Seagull Certificates (1 length 100 metres). Further information from Pay Office.

THE MORECAMBE BAY PRINTERS LTD., MORECAMBE.

The calendar of events for 1959 shows the range of entertainment on offer during a typical season at the Super Swimming Stadium.

13-year old Malcolm O'Neil made the most of his Junior Season Ticket in the summer of 1966, visiting the Super Swimming Stadium on sixteen occasions and not missing a day one week in June.

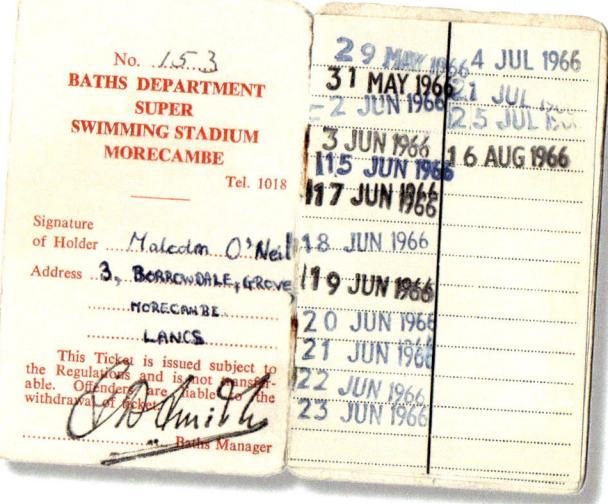

Baths Manager Glynn D. Smith came up with the idea of a Shiverers Club, a club so exclusive that only one person each year was granted membership – the first to enter the water at the beginning of each season. Competition was keen; in 1972 10-year old Kenneth Wilman was so determined to match his sister, who had won the previous year, he booked an early morning call for 5am. However, arriving at the stadium just before it opened he found he had been pipped by 11-year old Deborah Ward who had been waiting outside since 8am. She won a complimentary season ticket – as also did Kenneth who received one for his gallant attempt.

Blue Seagull certificates and badges were first issued in the early 1950s to all local children and holidaymakers who managed to 'swim unaided and self-propelled, from Deep to Shallow, one length of the Super Swimming Stadium'.

'SHIVERERS CLUB' AT THE BATHS

A 'CLUB' so exclusive that only one person can join each year was founded at Morecambe today.

It was the "Shiverers Club," – the idea of local baths manager Mr Glyn Smith. He decided that the first person to take a dip in the resort's open air swimming stadium each year, should be granted membership of the club.

"Should the same person be first each year the membership will be confined to one," he said with a laugh.

First to enter the water today was local journalist Miss Eileen Wood, aged 17, of Parliament - street, Morecambe. She took a quick dip in water which had a temperature of 48 degrees Farenheit.

But as she left the water shivering she was told that she could not be a full member of the club because she was not a member of the general public. She was granted honorary membership instead.

First full member of the club is Miss Gail Hodgson, 15, of Michaelson-avenue, Morecambe, who entered the water about 15 minutes after Eileen. Gail is studying at Lancaster Commercial College and is a former pupil of Morecambe Grammar School.

 **BOROUGH OF MORECAMBE AND HEYSHAM**
Baths Department

Super Swimming Stadium

This is to certify that

...........VIVIENNE LOVE...........

did on the ...TWENTYSECOND... day of ...AUGUST, 1974...
swim unaided and self-propelled, from Deep to Shallow, one length at the Super Swimming Stadium, one of the longest pools in Europe; and is hereby elected and accepted as a BLUE SEAGULL. Notice is Given to all swimmers and divers to give friendship and assistance to the person named hereon under pain of displeasure of all other Blue Seagulls.

Signed............
FROM THE HOME OF THE BLUE SEAGULL AND WHERE THE REGISTER OF MEMBERS IS KEPT.

Vivienne Love was fourteen when she gained her signed certificate and enamelled badge in August 1974, one of the last to be awarded before the stadium closed for good the following month.

The Remedial Department at the Super Swimming Stadium was opened in January 1952. Its equipment was second hand, having come from the indoor baths at Morecambe's Broadway Hotel which were closed down when the building was requisitioned for Government use at the beginning of World War Two. The treatments provided were intended to have preventative rather than curative effects and 'give a feeling of well-being to patients'.

Slipper baths were added soon afterwards. So called because of their shape, they became popular in Victorian and Edwardian England when the majority of working class houses had no bathing facilities other than a tin tub in front of the fire. Slipper baths were installed in municipal wash-houses to improve public health and hygiene, regular bathing having been shown to help prevent the spread of disease. Even in 1950s Morecambe many homes still lacked inside toilets and not all had a bathroom.

Although most boarding houses possessed a bathroom, its frequent use was discouraged by landladies and guests often found the door locked. A spokesman for Morecambe hoteliers defended this action saying: "If you don't lock the bathroom up they [the guests] will take baths every day."(!) For many years the stadium's slipper baths provided a valuable amenity and were well patronised by residents and visitors. However, by 1966 falling numbers and the fact that prices had barely changed since 1952, meant that the Remedial Department was losing around £2,000 a year and, despite some opposition, its closure was confirmed that September.

The piece of land between the stadium and the promenade was originally intended for a 15-hole 'putting green with bunkers'. Whilst this never materialised, an alternative version of the game called Crazy Golf later appeared in the triangular space adjacent to the western end of the stadium.

An advertisement included in the programme for the stadium's *Aqua-Cascades*.

Crazy Golf could be enjoyed by all ages and was a popular attraction during the 1950s and 1960s. Usually played on an artificial surface (in this case, wood) the game involved negotiating various obstacles such as ramps, tunnels and buildings, en route to each hole.

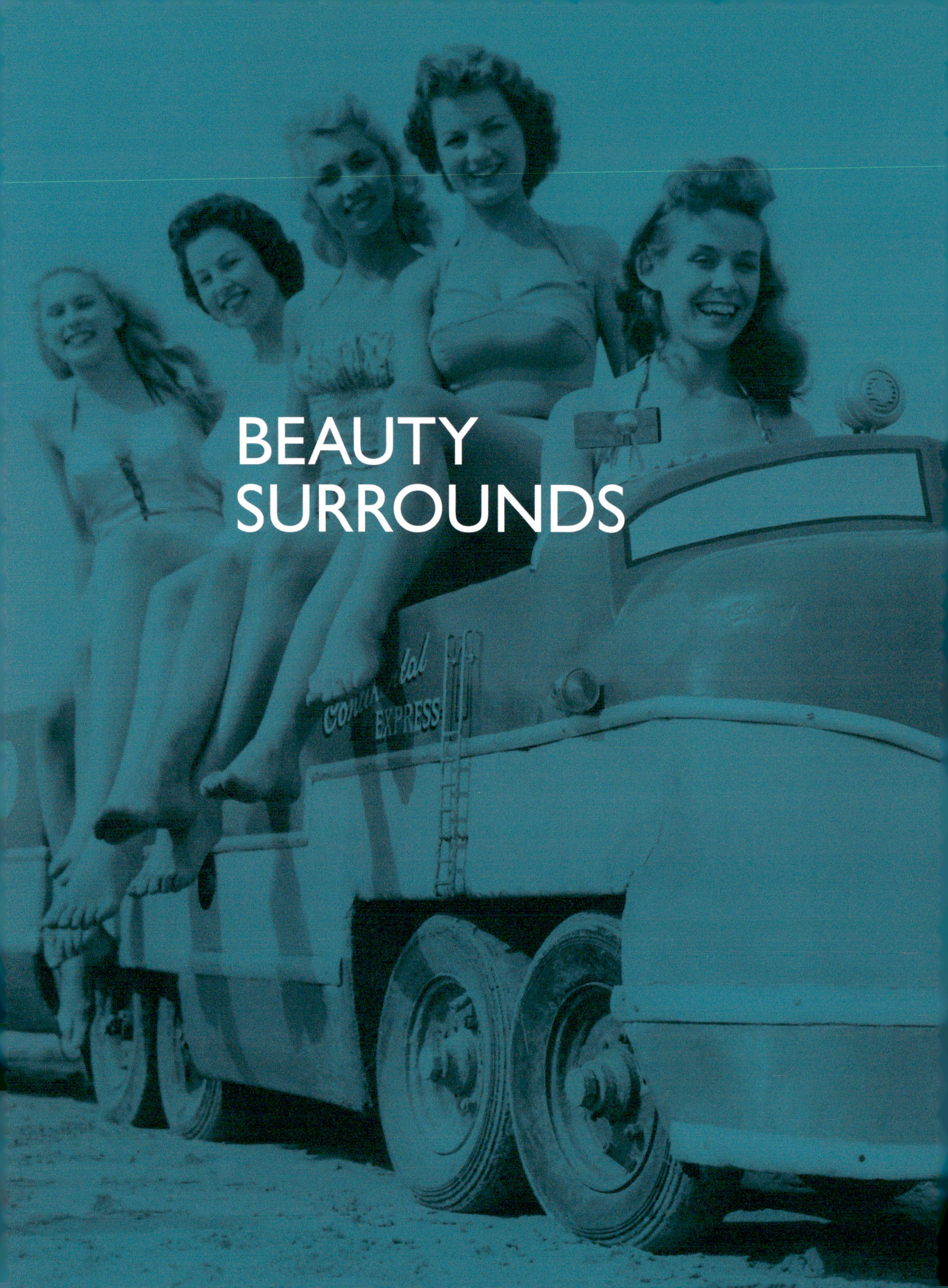
BEAUTY SURROUNDS

SIX

On a damp and overcast late summer afternoon in 1945 at Morecambe's Super Swimming Stadium, a young woman in a simple white bathing costume stepped forward to receive from the mayor a silver cup, seven guineas, a new swimsuit and a basket of fruit. The date was August 29th and the young woman was Lydia Reid, the first winner of the newly inaugurated National Bathing Beauty Competition.

The event had been the brainchild of Edwin M. Briggs, Publicity and Entertainments Manager for Morecambe and Heysham Corporation. Earlier in the year, as the war in Europe was coming to an end, he had approached Charles Eade, editor of the *Sunday Dispatch*, then Britain's biggest selling Sunday newspaper, with a proposition. Morecambe was planning to hold a beauty contest, similar to the *Daily Dispatch*'s pre-war quest for 'The Seaside Girl' and would he be interested in helping to organise such a competition on modest lines later that year to test the public's reaction? It would provide some much needed cheer after six years of austerity as well as giving a boost to Morecambe's economy – everyone loved a pretty girl, pretty girls would draw crowds, crowds would spend money.

The sight of a young woman in a swimsuit was not exactly a novel experience in Morecambe – it was, after all, a seaside resort, even in wartime. People mingled freely in the swimming stadium with no restrictions as to how and where they swam and sunbathed. The opening of anything water based seemed to require a mannequin parade of the latest fashions in swimwear; the Windsor Water Woollies girls had shown off their wares at the opening of the stadium in 1936 and there had been a similar event at the miniature marine pool on the promenade where, at the Bathing Belle Parade, 'some pretty and striking designs were displayed'.

None of these was a direct appraisal of the female form although this was an added bonus. In 1931, however, during the Summer Carnival week, people were startled by a new spectacle. According to the *Visitor*: 'Central Pier has never housed so much beauty as it did on Saturday afternoon, as in addition to the Carnival Queen Parade in robes, there was a parade of shapely girls in bathing costumes with Miss Louie Irish of Manchester chosen as the most shapely.' The protests were almost immediate, typified by the comment of one disapproving councillor who declared: "It is not decent to have a body of a young woman semi-nude exhibiting themselves in public", drawing responses asking what his expectations were when Morecambe acquired its new pool. Whatever he expected, in the summer of 1945 there would be dozens of young women in bathing suits, proudly parading around the stadium in front of thousands of people – and with full Council approval.

A foretaste of the excitement to come was reported in the *Visitor* of 25th August 1937. A beauty contest, sponsored by the *Daily Mail,* had been held at the Harbour Band Arena attracting a huge number of spectators. 'Nearly 3,000 deckchairs were occupied in the Arena and thousands of people, unable to obtain a seat, stood around the enclosure. Many bathers in the Super Swimming Stadium close by, deserted the swimming pool and crowded the top balcony of the Baths to get a bird's-eye view.' Some of the less confident girls, perhaps daunted by the size of the crowd, dropped out leaving fifteen, mainly holidaymakers, to parade in their swimsuits on that warm, sunny afternoon. The winner was Miss Dorothy Cowan, a shorthand typist from Leeds, persuaded to take part by her boyfriend who had read the advertising placards. Dorothy was described as 'a blue-eyed blonde, slim, vivacious, glowing with health, having graceful deportment, perfect teeth and an infectious smile'. Regrettably, the *Visitor* failed to record her reward for winning.

In 1945, having considered the Corporation's request, Charles Eade offered advice and encouragement; if the competition proved successful the *Sunday Dispatch* would be pleased to offer more substantial support in the hopes of boosting both the newspaper's circulation and the prosperity of Morecambe. Organisation fell to the Corporation's Publicity and Entertainments Department with much of the work being shouldered by Edwin Briggs' secretary, Miss Dorothy Fisher. The plan was to hold five preliminary heats at the Super Swimming Stadium culminating in a Grand Final for the heat winners. Entry was free and the only stipulation was that contestants must not be less than sixteen years of age. The first heat took place in brilliant sunshine on 25th July 1945, sandwiched between VE Day and VJ Day. It attracted fourteen entries and was won by 19-year old Mary Drummond from Glasgow, probably in Morecambe on holiday. She received a prize of two guineas and accommodation in the resort for the final. Vera Atkinson of Lancaster came second and Audrey Battersby of Morecambe was placed third. While the judges were pondering their decision spectators were treated to 'a Unique Spectacle of Springboard Diving' by Leon Marco and Ambrose Smith, 'International Exhibition Divers'. Despite the lack of publicity – only a small advertisement appeared in the *Visitor* the week before the contest – over 5,000 people turned up to watch.

The following week witnessed an even larger crowd at the stadium and a doubling of the number of entrants to thirty. Elsie Laycock of Lancaster emerged as the winner but for some reason did not participate in the final, her place being taken by Doreen Roper of Chesterfield who came second in the heat. Another Lancaster girl, Jean Dunster, triumphed in heat three in front of a record attendance of 6,208. Until then the adjudication had usually been performed by local worthies and RAF servicemen stationed in Morecambe but for heat four, won by June Rivers, a military nurse at Kirkham, the musical star Jessie Matthews was asked to be one of the judges. This began the trend of inviting whichever famous performers were appearing at the Winter

Gardens in the town that week to help select the winner, a decision which raised the profile of the competition and helped to attract even more spectators. In the last heat local girl Lydia Reid was placed second to Alice Tolley from Blackpool but the scores were so close that the judges, perhaps swayed by the partisan demands of the crowd, agreed she should also be one of the finalists.

The arrangements for the Grand Final were placed in the hands of the sub-committee (Bathing Beauty Competition) of the Publicity and Entertainments department and at its last meeting, the week before the event, the plans were revealed. A silver cup, inscribed 'Borough of Morecambe and Heysham Bathing Beauty Competition', which the recipient would hold for one year only, would be presented by the mayor along with other prizes; Windsor Water Woollies would be providing swimsuits as gifts for all finalists. Invited guests were to be treated to lunch at no more than four shillings per head. Schoolchildren would join the professional divers and swimmers in entertaining the spectators and be rewarded with a small memento for their efforts, for which £20 had been put aside.

Borough of Morecambe and Heysham

SUPER SWIMMING STADIUM

BATHING BEAUTY QUEEN CONTEST – FINAL

To-day (Wednesday), Aug. 29, at 3 p.m.

The British Film Star from Gainsborough Pictures –

MICHAEL RENNIE

has kindly agreed to act as Chairman of the Judges.

The Finalist will become the holder of a Cup (presented by the Morecambe and Heysham Corporation) for one year, and will receive a CASH PRIZE of £7 7s., also a SWIMSUIT presented by "Windsor Water Woollies" and BATHING WRAP by Messrs. Jephsons, Promenade, Morecambe.

ALL THE COMPETITORS WILL BE GIVEN A MEMENTO.

Photographs will appear in "The Sunday Dispatch."

If wet, this Parade will be held in Winter Gardens Ballroom.

Also Special Engagement of "THE AQUABATS"

Britain's Foremost Diving Team in a show of Grace, Thrills and Comedy.

HIGH AND ACROBATIC DIVING.

PRICE OF ADMISSION, 1/6. Seats at the Diving End, 6d. extra.

Advertisement from the *Visitor* 29th August 1945.

Michael Rennie, a leading film actor of the time, had been appointed as chair of the judging panel which was to include Norman Craig of Gaumont British Pictures and A.N. Other (who on the day turned out to be Denis Shipwright, a man with a colourful past in motor racing, politics and films, currently with the RAF). The judges would be aided by the Bathing Beauty sub-committee who had to 'note the amount of applause'. To add to the publicity, Jephsons were to display the Cup and prize swimsuit, along with the wrap they were supplying, in the window of their shop on the promenade.

The weather for the Grand Final on August 29th was atrocious. The torrential rain, however, did not dampen the enthusiasm of the 4,277 spectators, swathed in mackintoshes and huddled under umbrellas. Despite the offer of alternative accommodation from the Winter Gardens the organisers pressed ahead with the swimming stadium venue, possibly from reluctance to lose revenue or maybe because the military band that had been booked would not be allowed to play in the theatre. After the six finalists had bravely paraded around the pool the three judges were not long in deliberation before choosing 18-year old Lydia Reid as National Bathing Beauty Queen, a decision which, not surprisingly, went down well with the largely local audience. The mayor, Councillor George Bravin, presented Lydia with the silver cup, a new swimming costume, a basket of fruit and a cash prize of seven guineas, an amount witheringly derided by the *Visitor* as 'paltry'.

The six finalists in the 1945 National Bathing Beauty Competition, Doreen Roper, Alice Tolley, June Rivers, Lydia Reid, Jean Dunster and Mary Drummond lock arms and smile bravely for the photographer despite the chilly weather. No particular style of swimsuit or shoe prevailed and the girls have a natural appearance with few fussy accessories.

The winner of the first final in 1945 was 18-year old Lydia Reid, a Civil Service typist from Morecambe, seen here posing for a publicity photograph in her white satin swimsuit made specially for the contest by her mother.

The crowd went away wet but happy having enjoyed the entertainment, a glimpse of a famous film star and having seen their favourite win. After her memorable afternoon Lydia returned home with her prizes, insignificant by later standards though welcome after the privations of wartime, and to her day job as a Civil Service typist. Morecambe councillors were happy too; the competition had been a resounding financial success and, as a bonus, the proceedings had been filmed by the Gaumont British News Service and would be shown in cinemas throughout the country, providing Morecambe with invaluable advertising at no cost to the town.

Buoyed by the public's enthusiastic response, the organisers saw a bright future for the contest. Next year's competition would be bigger and better. With increased publicity, contestants were drawn from a wider area and ten weekly heats were held in Morecambe. In two of these the judges could not agree on a winner and it was decided that two girls from each should go forward to the final. The *Sunday Dispatch* assumed the role of sponsor for the competition, donating a solid silver rose bowl to be presented to the winner (to keep), while Morecambe Corporation, perhaps stung by the *Visitor*'s criticism, raised the cash prize to £100. This was good news for June Rivers, one of the previous year's finalists now working in Manchester. While no doubt disappointed not to have won the inaugural contest, she qualified for the 1946 Grand Final by winning the first of the heats. This time she emerged triumphant, defeating the eleven other girls to take the title and the greatly enhanced prize money.

Just like 1945 it was wretched weather for the final with a chilly wind and heavy showers. Fortunately, the rain held off for a brief spell when the finalists paraded in front of the three judges – George Formby (comedian and film star), Charles Eade (editor of the *Sunday Dispatch*) and, perhaps a strange choice, Professor C.E.M. Joad (Philosophy don and radio broadcasting personality, one of the first academic celebrities). During the afternoon additional entertainment for the 7,000 spectators was provided by the

The top three in a 1946 heat – Pamela Summers, Susan Williams and Jeanette Fyfe – are congratulated by Suzette Tarri, a popular Cockney stage and radio comedienne of the time. Along with fellow judge, Irish singer Cavan O'Connor, she was on the bill at the Winter Gardens that week. The *Visitor* thought it worth noting that they 'made the awards on their own observations in contrast to the previous week when the judges were largely guided by the applause of the crowd'.

The programme photographs of the 1946 finalists have a strangely artificial air with generally more elaborate hairstyles and a proliferation of flowery accessories.

Actor and comedian George Formby is flanked by the 1946 winner, June Rivers and the runner-up (for the second time) Jean Dunster, with Charles Eade, editor of the *Sunday Dispatch*, standing behind. At this point, George was heard to quip: "This is what I call turned out nice again." When June qualified by winning the first heat she was a nurse in a military hospital on the Fylde but by the time of the final she had become a model working for a chain of Manchester cinemas.

This small agricultural display presents an unfortunate juxtaposition of venues; the bathing beauty pageants held at the swimming stadium were likened by their detractors to cattle shows. An alternative view, widely held at the time, was expressed by the mayor, Councillor Raymond Penhale, in his after dinner speech following the 1958 final. "I like to see girls in bathing costumes. If a girl is endowed with physical attributes which are attractive and outstanding, why should she not exploit them in a right way? – like a man having a flair for the Stock Exchange makes full use of it. The Corporation will never be associated with a competition unless it is clean and dignified and well run."

Band of the South Lancashire Regiment, the diving displays and comedy routines of the Aquabats and mannequin parades of bathing fashions past, present and future by Windsor Water Woollies. A total of 57,133 spectators attended the ten heats and final resulting in record takings of £4,242 for the stadium.

Although most people were pleased with the success of the event, there were dissenting voices. A local churchman, finding the whole idea rather distasteful, wrote: "It seems a curious thing that a young woman can walk around before thousands of people as near naked as the law allows in order to have her physical points assessed as if she were some sort of prize animal at a cattle show." This view, more forcibly expressed in a later era, was not widely held at the time and was largely ignored in the clamour for an even more ambitious show.

With one exception all the finalists in 1945 and 1946 were from the north of the country. In an attempt to widen the scope of the 1947 event, and to ensure that the word 'National' in the title National Bathing Beauty Competition was completely justified, it was decided to introduce a photographic element as a preliminary to the

Out of the thousands of photographic entries which poured into the offices of the *Sunday Dispatch* each spring, four winners were chosen to represent England, Wales, Scotland and Ireland. The photographers responsible for the winning portraits also earned themselves small prizes. In 1954 Eira Roberts became Miss Wales and joined 39 other contestants in the Grand Final in Morecambe.

On 28th May 1947, in brilliant sunshine and under cloudless blue skies, over 4,500 people turned up to see Stan Laurel and Oliver Hardy choose May Hart (left), a 26-year old Irish born hairdresser, as winner of the first heat of that year's competition. Billed as 'Hollywood's Greatest Comedy Couple' Laurel and Hardy were appearing twice nightly for a week at the Winter Gardens, seats 1/6 to 6/-.

'SUNDAY DISPATCH' BATHING BEAUTY COMPETITION.
Miss Eira Roberts, Barry, Glamorgan, winner of the title "MISS WALES" in the photographic section.

fifteen personal appearance heats planned for Morecambe. From the thousands who sent in their pictures to the *Sunday Dispatch,* four winners were selected, one each from England, Scotland, Wales and Ireland, increasing the number taking part in the final to nineteen. At the same time the organisers, wanting to keep the Morecambe name prominent, were determined that local talent should not be overlooked. It became a tradition that the first heat held at the swimming stadium each year would be limited to young women living within fifteen miles of Morecambe Town Hall. The winner became Miss Morecambe and received automatic entry to the Grand Final; the losers were free to try their luck against girls from elsewhere in any of the subsequent heats.

Responding to the event's increasing popularity, Morecambe Corporation dipped further into its purse, upping the winner's cheque to £500. And popular it certainly was; thousands flocked to see the shows. Nearly every week that summer set new attendance records and for one heat in July the gates were closed half an hour before the scheduled start with 7,300 people packed inside the stadium. The nineteen finalists were drawn from a range of occupations – models, shop girls, office workers and a Land Army girl 'who travelled all the way from Berkshire to Morecambe to win her heat'. Despite all efforts, there was still a bias towards entries from northern England, especially the North-West and Yorkshire, the traditional source of Morecambe's holiday trade.

In contrast to the previous two years the weather for the 1947 Grand Final was warm and sunny. Ever more ambitious, the organisers had booked the Oslo born film actress

In 1948 Wilfred Pickles and his wife Mabel, popular radio stars of the time, chose Pamela Bayliss from Northern Ireland as the winner. That year ten of the twenty finalists came from North-West England, despite attempts to make the National Bathing Beauty Contest truly national.

Greta Gynt, one of J. Arthur Rank's leading ladies, to chair the judges – although she nearly didn't appear. On the day of the final she was scheduled to fly from Stavanger in Norway via Northolt and land at Blackpool airport from where a fast car with police escort would whisk her to Morecambe. An unexpected delay at Northolt, however, meant a change of plan. A light plane was hired at Blackpool and after a circuit over the stadium it landed on Middleton Sands from where Greta was driven to Morecambe, arriving with just a few minutes to spare. Once she had got her breath back, she and the other judges, Charles Eade and Charles Shadwell, former head of BBC music, chose June Mitchell from Birmingham as that year's National Bathing Beauty Queen.

Having found what appeared to be a winning formula, the contest for 1948 followed a similar pattern, apart from the weather which was once again described as 'appalling throughout the season'. Crowds still turned up, with a record 7,500 filling the stadium in early August. June Mitchell was invited back to be one of the judges at the Grand Final, using her experience to help radio broadcaster Wilfred Pickles, his wife Mabel and Charles Eade select the winner from the twenty contestants. For the first time the title went across the Irish Sea, to Pamela Bayliss from Lisburn, County Antrim.

The continuing success of Morecambe's Bathing Beauty Contest had not gone unnoticed by potential rival organisations, a number of which were considering starting their own versions. One of these was Mecca Dancing owned by Eric Morley. In 1948 he wrote to Charles Eade saying he was planning to run a national competition entitled Miss Great Britain and would the *Sunday Dispatch* be interested in sponsoring it. Eade replied that he was already involved with Morecambe's contest but why didn't Morley join them and create an even larger competition? Morley agreed and in 1949 twelve heats for the National Bathing Beauty Queen were also staged in Mecca dance halls throughout the country, starting in Belfast in January when representatives of all three sponsors braved Irish Sea gales to witness the event. From the twelve Mecca winners three were chosen to appear in the Grand Final in Morecambe's Super Swimming Stadium. One of these, Elaine Pryce of Bolton, who had won her heat in Manchester's Ritz Ballroom, went on to take the £500 first prize and an invitation to travel to Sicily in September as Miss Great Britain to represent the country in the Miss Europe contest.

For the following year's contest the first prize was doubled to £1,000, an astonishing figure given that it was several times the average UK annual salary in 1950. Second and third prizes remained at £100 and £50 respectively, while the other finalists each received £10. It was a reflection of how large the competition had become in such a short space of time; was it only five years since the winner received seven guineas? Thousands entered via the heats in Morecambe's swimming stadium and Mecca ballrooms, the photographic competition and from a new venture – the 'Court of Queens'. Backed by commercial and industrial concerns, three more finalists appeared in the form of Miss Lyons, the Candy Queen and the Mecca Princess.

Spectators were advised that seats for the Grand Final that year could be booked for five shillings which, coupled with a sixpenny programme, could make quite a dent in a visitor's holiday cash, but still the stadium was packed. From the 23 finalists the judges – Jimmy Edwards and Joy Nichols, stars of the radio programme *Take It from*

Elaine Pryce from Bolton, holding the *Sunday Dispatch* rose bowl while posing on the ten metre diving board, was the first winner to come from Eric Morley's Mecca ballroom heats. She briefly took the title 'Miss Great Britain' while representing the country in the Miss Europe contest.

Violet Pretty, the first to win £1,000 in 1950, chats with judges Charles Eade, Jimmy Edwards and Joy Nichols, with runner-up Marlene Dee (the following year's winner) and third placed Margaret Mansergh looking on. By the age of eighteen, Violet had already been successful in the beauty business, winning £1,800 in prize money over the previous two years. Realising that more than a pretty face and good figure was required to fulfil her ambition of a career in films, she invested her money in drama lessons and, while playing Aladdin in pantomime, was spotted by the Rank Organisation and offered her cherished dream of a life on the big screen.

Here – picked the aptly named Violet Pretty from Birmingham as the winner. Although this was the 18-year old's first appearance in the final, she had been in Morecambe the previous year as a Mecca semi-finalist and, learning from her experience, had been motivated to try again. On returning home to her native city she was met at New Street Station by cheering crowds and driven in a Rolls Royce to a civic reception hosted by the Lord Mayor. Violet used her winnings wisely, taking lessons in elocution, singing, dancing and acting. These paid off when she was offered a seven year contract by the Rank Organisation. She went on to enjoy a long and successful film career under the stage name of Anne Heywood.

Throughout the 1950s the contest continued to grow despite competition from other similar events. Charles Eade proudly claimed, in the foreword to the 1952 programme, that Morecambe's National Bathing Beauty Contest "has grown in size and importance and today it stands supreme as the greatest competition of its kind in this country. Indeed, in some ways, it is the greatest in the world". In 1953 Butlins joined the list of sponsors, holding heats throughout the summer season at its holiday camps in Ayr, Clacton, Dublin, Filey, Pwhelli and Skegness to add six more finalists to the mix. All the Mecca heat winners were invited to the final instead of just three so that with all those from the Morecambe heats and the winners of the photographic competition there were regularly more than forty girls in the stadium for the Grand Final.

The £1,000 first prize continued to be attractive but perhaps an equal draw was the chance to become Miss World. In 1951 Eric Morley of Mecca, with the backing of the *Sunday Dispatch*, had inaugurated an international beauty contest in London as part of the Festival of Britain – the beginnings of Miss World. It was decided that, in the future, Morecambe's winner would be the United Kingdom's representative, bearing the title Miss Great Britain. This began to appear on the winner's sash, firstly in small print and then taking pride of place – Miss Great Britain became synonymous with Morecambe.

Although supposedly from all walks of life, the young women who entered the competition came increasingly from the world of modelling and professional beauty. An article in the *Daily Herald* of June 1956 speaks of a 'merry-go-round' where the same faces appear at contests all over the country. For some, beauty contests provided a living during the season. One interviewee had entered Miss GB several times over a summer, coming second on three occasions and earning £5 each time; another had collected three prizes in one week – as a finalist for Miss GB (£20), for Miss Blackpool (£25) and for Miss English Rose, Southport (£10). A glance at the Miss GB programmes of that era bears this out with the same names occurring repeatedly in the finals. In 1951 for example, 10 out of 26 finalists had been there before and in 1956 almost half of the 43 finalists were repeats.

With so many appearing together so often a kind of camaraderie developed among the girls despite their seeming rivalry, leading Eric Morley to comment: "And that is the trouble with British girls. They aren't vicious enough. And they haven't enough sex appeal. You can quote me on that." The competitions at the Super Swimming Stadium were always held to be friendly affairs with most finalists taking advantage of the Corporation's offer of accommodation for Grand Final week at the Morecambe Bay

Photographers perch on the edge of the platform while taking shots of the contestants. With no thought of health or safety, spectators take up more precarious positions in an attempt to get a better view. Note the lack of a number thirteen – this superstitious habit finally ended in 1952.

The 1952 winner Doreen Dawne enjoys a joke with judges Beryl and George Formby with, on the left, Cesar Romero and, on the right, Charles Eade, escorting the runners-up, Brenda Mee and Sylvia Jenkins. The girls bravely attempt to smile, shivering in their swimsuits, while the others seem more suitably dressed for a typical August afternoon in Morecambe.

In the 1950s huge numbers queued up for what was deemed good family entertainment. Janet Elliott (daughter of the then Baths Superintendent, George Campbell Cooper) recalled how she and a friend were entrusted with the job of going among the crowds to sell programmes at 6d each, earning themselves 1/- for every 100 sold.

The swimming pool was cleared only for special events such as the actual Miss GB final so that these heat contestants were subjected to scrutiny, not just by the judges but also by male swimmers determined to get a much closer view.

For many years the finalists completed their journey along the promenade to the Super Swimming Stadium in horse-drawn landaus. Their arrival would be eagerly awaited by the crowds queuing to enter the stadium.

Holiday Camp in Heysham, where they were chaperoned by the solicitous Mrs Hughes who 'catered for their every need, even to the extent of ironing their pretty dresses'. (To help preserve this goodwill between competitors, in 1960, a local resident, Mrs D.P. Rouse, donated a small prize, to be awarded to 'Miss Conviviality', the contestant who the other finalists voted for as the most popular among them during their week's stay.)

The demands on contestants and winners in the early 1950s were relatively minor. The organisers prided themselves on the fact that this competition, unlike many others, did not tie the winner down to any subsequent contract. As Charles Eade observed: "Complete freedom is given them to do whatever they wish with their prize money. Previous winners have spent it to further ambitions in films or on the stage or for a vocation they have set their hearts on. Others have been able to marry, buy a house and settle down. It gives me great happiness to know this contest can help these young women on the threshold of life."

At this time, and indeed up to the end of the 1960s, the Grand Final was a relatively simple affair despite the pages of detailed instructions sent out to finalists beforehand. Those from out of town were at liberty to enjoy the hospitality offered free of charge by the Corporation for the entire week of the final, including visits to the theatre and trips around the area. Everyone had to be present on the Tuesday evening to attend a dinner or similar function in full evening attire followed by a briefing session back at the holiday camp. On the Wednesday, after a restful night's beauty sleep, they had to be ready to leave around 1.30pm for the stadium. For many years the transport was in the form of horse-drawn landaus which obviously attracted public attention and their arrival was often captured on film so the girls were advised to 'look their best' on the journey.

Arrival at the stadium was timed for around 2.00pm to give the girls time to change into swimsuits for the parade and judging. They were advised that bikinis and boned costumes were definitely banned and that inspections would be carried out to check for 'artificial aids or attachments'. Personality could be expressed through make-up, hair decorations and shoes! At the appointed time, usually about 3.00pm, the ever efficient Miss Dorothy Fisher ushered the young women from the changing rooms with last minute instructions ringing in their ears: "Keep in the correct order and at the prescribed intervals, walk confidently, turn at the right times, display your number clearly, don't hide anyone else's, smile, don't sign autographs, don't stop for unofficial photographs, speak to the judges if they speak to you" – all while walking round the edge of a swimming pool wearing high heels and subject to the gaze and comments of the public.

The redoubtable Miss Dorothy Fisher handing out a numbered disc and last minute instructions to Drene Hardcastle from Liverpool at a heat in 1955. Miss Fisher was responsible for the smooth running of the competition from its inception until the end of its time in the Super Swimming Stadium.

Two posters advertising the competition. That for the final in 1955 calls it the 'National Bathing Beauty Contest' and gives the sponsorship of the *Sunday Dispatch* pride of place whereas that for 1956 names it 'Miss Great Britain', stresses the money to be won and all four sponsors share equal billing.

The contestants themselves helped promote the final, making appearances in unexpected locations, as here, in swimsuits, on the shores of Lake Windermere ...

... or, more conventionally dressed, at Forton (Lancaster) Service Station on the M6.

Then there was the waiting with bated breath to see if your number was called to still be in contention. Depending on the number of competitors there could be several of these elimination rounds until finally the judges selected their winner and runners-up. The not so lucky losers could then relax and look forward to their consolation prizes plus their travelling expenses (a third class rail return fare until its replacement by second class in 1956). The first, second and third prize winners had to work a little harder for their money; there were the numerous photographic poses to be struck for newspapers, film crews and Morecambe Corporation's Publicity Department as well as presentations at local theatres. (Miss GB also had to make herself available for the Miss World contest later in the year.) All contestants could enjoy rounding off the day at a reception with the mayor and then dinner at one of Morecambe's leading hotels. For those with energy to spare this would be followed by a more informal night of dancing and drinks back at the holiday camp.

The smooth running of the contest was interrupted in 1958. In 1957 the *Sunday Dispatch* had announced that it would be ceasing its association with Miss GB the following year because of a change of policy. It was clear to Morecambe Corporation that Butlins and Mecca Dancing would follow suit. Eric Morley was about to fulfil his ambition of running his own rival contest, one which would elect a Miss United Kingdom who would usurp Morecambe's Miss GB as the country's representative in Miss World (another Morley enterprise). The partnership was dissolved; for the first time since 1945 the Corporation was on its own.

Persistence eventually paid off for drama student Leila Williams who took the title in 1957 at her third attempt. While balancing on a boulder-strewn Morecambe shore, she holds the last of the *Sunday Dispatch* trophies, the newspaper having decided to end its sponsorship of the competition. The following year Leila gave up her life on the beauty circuit, saying: "The beauty queen game is hard going. The strain is bad enough on the way to the top. It's terrifying trying to stay there. I won £3,000 in two years and I consider that I earned it. I sold my swimsuits in aid of charity. None of them had ever been wet apart from visits to the laundry. I've always been terrified of swimming pools. I've never swum in any." Leila went on to find fame in television, becoming the first female presenter of the BBC children's programme *Blue Peter*.

Opposite: Abandoned not just by the *Sunday Dispatch* but by Mecca and Butlins as well, Morecambe Corporation chose to go it alone in organising the 1958 competition. From a slightly reduced number of finalists (35) the judges selected Christine Mayo of Abergele as the winner (seen here with a silver trophy presented by the Corporation) and Marilyn Davies of Stockport and Dawn Read of Derby as second and third prize-winners.

To ensure wide and favourable coverage in the press, numerous invitations and complimentary tickets were issued.

The Super Swimming Stadium and Miss GB were of prime importance among the attractions of Morecambe and figured widely in publicity for the resort.

On the cover of the 1951 brochure for Morecambe and Heysham, Violet Pretty's image emphasises the bathing beauty competition as contributing to the enjoyment of a holiday in the resort along with the 'golden sands and sparkling blue sea'.

This shot of Margery Giles, Drene Hardcastle and Elizabeth Wilkinson, taken at a heat in 1955 and appearing in the resort's brochure for 1956, was typical of the time, using pretty girls to hold out the promise of a fun-filled holiday.

Morecambe's attractions, especially its Super Swimming Stadium, were on display to a wide audience when the 1960 film *The Entertainer* was released. The 1959 Miss GB final provided a backdrop for the scenes shot at the stadium, with many of the contestants, together with the judging panel chaired by McDonald Hobley, appearing in the film.

Laurence Olivier, as fading music hall comedian Archie Rice, takes on the role of compere for the Miss GB final. Shirley Anne Field, as Tina, replaced one of the actual competitors, losing out to the winner (on film as in real life) Valerie Martin.

1958 saw a slightly reduced line-up in the final; there were no photographic entrants but the Corporation, determined that the contest should not lapse, had done its best to replace the Butlins and Mecca heat winners with young women who had won beauty contests in independent dance halls and civic halls and at county shows and festivals throughout the British Isles. To compensate for the loss of a place at the Miss World final, the winner was promised a screen test by Granada TV.

Having shown that it was perfectly capable of running the competition by itself, Morecambe Corporation set to with a will to find sponsorship for the following year to guarantee financial stability. The first to sign up was the beauty products firm, Goya Ltd. Heat winners went home laden with cosmetics and perfumes and the overall winner was presented with the Goya statuette rather than the more usual silver cup or bowl. Another major benefactor was British European Airways who flew the successful Miss GB on a whistle-stop tour of the British Isles. In 1962 Fred Pontin joined the list of sponsors and finalists were invited to stay even further out of town at his Middleton Tower Holiday Camp.

The rewards for the contestants steadily increased, both for the light-hearted amateurs and for those who treated it as a profession. Typical of the former is the woman quoted in a 2003 *Reflections* section of the *Morecambe Guardian* who took part in the early 1960s. "During summer holidays from training college in London I entered this

Morecambe and Wise with the 1965 winner, Diane Westbury. Ernie holds the Goya statuette which became the main award when the company became major sponsors in 1959. Diane wears the Miss GB sash and cradles her own personal rose bowl.

Miss GB 1968, Yvonne Ormes, travelled far and wide from her Nantwich home during her year's reign, creating publicity for the competition and the resort of Morecambe. One of her more glamorous assignments took her to Florida, and a visit to Miami's Seaquarium.

and other such contests and in spite of their political incorrectness now, can only remember them with affection. We had a lot of fun. To win a heat of a prestigious competition like Miss Great Britain was equal to six weeks spent in a rock factory or café; in an eight week summer break I could win enough to give me spending money at college for a whole year."

For the big winners prizes ran into thousands of pounds. Along with the trophies and cash, they enjoyed foreign holidays (some with 'work' attached), flights, luxury cruises, designer clothes, diamond watches, luggage, beauty products, furs, shoes and access to modelling, film and TV careers. As the prizes and sponsors proliferated so did the demands on the girls. No longer could the lucky winner smile gratefully, bank her cheque then go home, kick off her heels and relax – Miss GB was becoming a full time job. Always bearing in mind her role as an 'ambassadress', she travelled the length and breadth of the country to model clothes, open stores, judge contests, present awards and spread the good name of her sponsors. As the embodiment of British health and beauty, she journeyed abroad, often to trade fairs and usually accompanied by the ever-dependable Miss Fisher whose organisational skills smoothed their passage. The name of Morecambe and Heysham was spread far and wide.

By the late 1960s Morecambe and Miss GB had settled into a steady relationship, the winners being showered with prizes (albeit with strings attached) and Morecambe Corporation reaping the rewards of a healthy income from the crowds the contest attracted. The Publicity Department saw the advent of television coverage as a step towards even greater things for the town and the competition. In 1970 Yorkshire TV

Viewed from the balcony, the 1970 finalists line up before the judges, special guests and TV cameras, preparatory to having their number cut from 27 to 16. The attendance appears considerably reduced compared with the huge crowds which packed the stadium in earlier years, perhaps an indication of the waning appeal of the contest or possibly because the winner would not actually be chosen that day.

arrived on the scene to experiment with filming the proceedings. In fact 1970 was experimental in several ways; the final extended over a two-day period with three swimsuited rounds on the Tuesday to reduce the contestants from 28 to 16 and, following a re-allocation of numbers, a round in evening wear on the Wednesday with a final round back in swimsuits for the best six – the whole process recorded on a multiplicity of coloured forms and described by several judges as 'complicated'.

1972 saw transmission of the Yorkshire TV filmed contest go nationwide at the peak viewing time of 8.00pm on the Wednesday evening of the final. By now the competition itself had evolved even further in order to provide more interest for the viewer. Still held over two days, it now included a round in casual wear (minis, maxis, trouser suits, hot pants – basically whatever contestants pleased) held on the Tuesday morning in the gardens outside the Super Swimming Stadium. This was followed in the afternoon by the traditional bathing beauty parade inside the stadium. Bikinis were now permitted, probably because many one-piece swimsuits had so much cut away that it was hard to tell the difference. Bizarrely, the instructions stated that tights were not allowed in this section. The third and final round took place on the Wednesday afternoon at the Winter Gardens when the girls donned their evening gowns to parade before the judges. While the marks for all the rounds were totted up and the judges held their final deliberations, there was a quick costume change into swimsuits for the verdict. The winner was presented, not just with a sash declaring her to be Miss GB and National Bathing Beauty, but with the full regalia of a fur-trimmed cloak and sparkling crown of a typical beauty queen.

The week's stay at a holiday camp for the finalists had long since been replaced by two or three days at the Mayfair Hotel in Morecambe itself. This may have been slightly more luxurious but it was certainly not relaxing; not only were there now three different types of competition to undergo but each of the rounds had to be carefully rehearsed beforehand to ensure there were no glitches when the cameras rolled for the real thing.

In 1973 angry scenes erupted outside the Winter Gardens when the doors remained resolutely shut at the advertised time for the televised final. When the tired, hungry and mutinous crowd was finally admitted some sixty minutes late, the organisers explained that the whole proceedings were running four and a half hours behind schedule. The heavy rain of the previous day had forced the cancellation of the filming of the casual wear section which had to then take place that very morning thus pushing rehearsal time for the final parade into the afternoon – in fact while the impatient crowd had been stuck outside the theatre. Rehearsal was necessary, they said, otherwise "the girls wouldn't have known what they were doing" and the television coverage would have been spoiled – a far cry from the early days when a quick change into a swimsuit, a totter round the pool and a smile at the judges was all that was required.

The final sixteen from the 1970 competition parade in evening wear on the stage of Morecambe's Winter Gardens theatre.

After her crowning in the Winter Gardens, the 1970 winner, Kathleen Winstanley of Wigan, poses in full regalia with runner-up Kathleen O'Neill and third placed Carolyn Moore perched beside her on the elaborate throne. Returning the following year to crown her successor, Kathleen expressed her regret about the direction in which the competition was heading, saying that all the TV cameras and numerous re-takes had turned it into "a fairground sideshow instead of a beauty contest".

The new format coupled with the demands of television to keep to a tight schedule meant that the number of finalists had to be restricted; semi-finals were held to ensure that this number was now sixteen and the date of the final itself was often pushed back into September. As a reward the girls were now able to view their performance on the screen. Long before the advent of home video recorders this meant watching as it was transmitted in the evening after the final. In 1972 colour sets were specially hired and installed in the Town Hall so that the finalists and their guests could relax with cocktails and see the show before progressing to the celebration banquet at the Midland Hotel. Next morning the majority of competitors would return home, leaving the new Miss GB to begin her reign fulfilling her obligations to appear at various Morecambe venues, meet the press and spend a rather lonely night at the hotel before flying away on her BEA tour of the British Isles the following day.

Despite some loss of control over their competition, Morecambe councillors were, on the whole, happy to support it and regarded the television coverage as excellent publicity for the town. Out in the real world, however, changes were happening which were to have a serious impact on the contest. Women's horizons were broadening; increased education and employment opportunities meant they were no longer tied

1973 was the last time the Super Swimming Stadium was used for the Grand Final parade of bathing beauties. Atrocious weather made the umbrellas a necessity rather than a mere accessory as the girls posed in a selection of colourful costumes but without their customary white stilettos. The following afternoon saw Gay Spink (front left) take the title Miss GB; her mother Betty had been a finalist in 1947 and 1948 and her twin sister Zoë reached the final in 1974.

Competitors arrive in vintage cars at the Promenade Gardens for the delayed daywear section of the 1973 final.

to domesticity and the typing pool – it became possible to earn a reasonable wage. Prize money from beauty competitions, although welcome, was no longer such a life-enhancing opportunity.

Attitudes were also changing; many people (men included) were expressing distaste at the idea of women demeaning themselves by parading 'semi-naked before the male gaze' to win a little money. In 1970 even Alan Whicker, one of the judges at the Miss GB final, declared that (despite being ostensibly a bathing beauty contest) "there was too much bathing costume … they all look plastic" and he would prefer to see the girls in street clothes! Later that same year at the Miss World contest in London a group of women staged a demonstration (banners, vocal protests and flour bombs) to draw the attention of a wider audience to the inequalities between the sexes and the exploitation of women for male enjoyment.

During the early 1970s there was little acknowledgement of these matters by those planning the Miss GB contests but practical problems had started to emerge. The Super Swimming Stadium had become run down and shabby and concerns had arisen regarding its safety with parts of the terraces declared dangerous and excluded from public use. The final blow fell in early 1974 when it was decided that it would be impossible to open the stadium that spring. It had already lost its starring role as the centrepiece of the Miss GB show, which it had now ceded to the Winter Gardens, but this was effectively the termination of its connection with the contest. Hasty rearrangements resulted in swimwear parades taking place outdoors in the Harbour Band Arena that year (or indoors in the Winter Gardens in very poor weather) apart from a few heats in July and August when the stadium briefly reopened. After nearly three decades, it was the end of an era – the link between Miss Great Britain and the Super Swimming Stadium was broken. The competition had outgrown its original concept and would take on a new life after the sad demise of its birthplace.

Winners of the National Bathing Beauty and Miss Great Britain Contests at Morecambe's Super Swimming Stadium 1945-1973

Year	Winner	Place	Year	Winner	Place
1945	Lydia Reid	Morecambe	1960	Eileen Sheridan	Walton-on-Thames
1946	June Rivers	Manchester	1961	Libby Walker	Blackpool
1947	June Mitchell	Birmingham	1962	Joy Black	Dumfries
1948	Pamela Bayliss	Lisburn	1963	Gillian Taylor	Cheadle
1949	Elaine Pryce	Bolton	1964	Carole Redhead	Poulton-le-Fylde
1950	Violet Pretty	Birmingham	1965	Diane Westbury	Altrincham
1951	Marlene Dee	Henley-on-Thames	1966	Carole Fletcher	Southport
1952	Doreen Dawne	London	1967	Jennifer Gurley	Sale
1953	Brenda Mee	Derby	1968	Yvonne Ormes	Nantwich
1954	Patricia Butler	Hoylake	1969	Wendy George	Derby
1955	Jennifer Chimes	Leamington Spa	1970	Kathleen Winstanley	Wigan
1956	Iris Waller	Gateshead	1971	Carolyn Moore	Nantwich
1957	Leila Williams	Walsall	1972	Elizabeth Robinson	Nottingham
1958	Christina Mayo	Abergele	1973	Gay Spink	Halifax
1959	Valerie Martin	Blackburn			

Programmes went up in price over time from 3d (just over 1p) in 1946 to 16p in 1973. The contents increased in line with the number of contestants and the amount of advertising – from a single piece in praise of the Super Swimming Stadium, through a series publicising other Morecambe attractions, then including adverts for local businesses and eventually full page spreads for the big sponsors and other national brands keen to associate with Miss GB.

A WINNING FORMULA

What did it take to become a winner of the coveted Miss Great Britain title?

The simple answer is that she had to appeal to the various subjective opinions of the judges, drawn from the ranks of current celebrities and representatives of the sponsors. To help the adjudicators, often with little experience of the task in hand, they were provided with a list of criteria which the winner should fulfil.

She was to be a young woman of at least sixteen years of age and no more than twenty-five (although the upper age limit occasionally varied) with the following attributes:
- a beautifully proportioned figure
- facial beauty
- deportment and an ability to maintain her poise at all times
- grooming ie. cleanliness, well-kept hair, smart accessories
- healthy, blemish free skin
- a happy, lively personality
- an air of maturity and responsibility as she would be an 'ambassadress' (added when this became a part of Miss GB's role)

At the Grand Final, each judge was presented with a rosette to wear.

All judges were issued with printed advice – generally followed but sometimes beyond their comprehension.

Not all judges took their responsibilities seriously. Many comedians, perhaps unsurprisingly, saw their role as crowd-pleasers as more important, injecting slapstick routines to lighten the proceedings. Other entertainers took the opportunity to make fun of their rivals or more serious-minded 'friends', playing jokes which occasionally misfired. At the 1963 final, as TV presenter Hughie Green leapt to the rostrum in an attempt to kiss the winner, he received a gentle nudge from the singer David Whitfield which resulted in his entering the pool with a resounding splash. Unfortunately, Hughie was not amused and threatened to sue Morecambe Corporation over the cost of his expensive watch and mohair suit, eventually settling for £25 to pay for the dry-cleaning. David tried to play it down, saying: "What's £25 between friends? It's Hughie's birthday on Sunday so he can have another suit on me as a present." The memory lingered a little longer in the minds of the Corporation; at the 1965 final, the mayor welcomed

For the twenty-first final, in 1965, the very first winner, Lydia Reid (now Johnson) was invited back to be one of the adjudicators. She is seen here (front row, third from right) with fellow judges (from left to right) comedians Ernie Wise and Eric Morecambe, singer Susan Maughan, Chairman of the London Palladium Leslie Macdonnell, comedienne Hylda Baker and singer David Whitfield.

back the popular David Whitfield but claimed that he had been asked by the Borough Treasurer to suggest to David that: "If by any chance he gets an uncontrollable urge to push somebody in the pool this afternoon, would he please pick someone who isn't wearing a fifty quid suit and a £100 watch. Our finances have apparently not recovered since the last time he was on the judging panel!"

Occasionally, those tasked with awarding prizes running into thousands of pounds were tempted to take their share by overindulging in the hospitality on offer. In 1974, the new Miss GB, Marilyn Ward, in her speech at the post-final banquet, thanked the judges for "remaining sober throughout. Some of the girls will know what I am talking about".

A few celebrities were unable to handle any scoring system involving numbers (introduced to cope with the different types of round for the television coverage). As one 1970 finalist commented: "Even the simplest of systems could confuse a judge." After that year's contest, a panel member declared it to be "too complicated", even with the explanatory booklet. Two others admitted their surprise on finding that girls they had fully expected to be in the final six had already been eliminated. At the post-final banquet a petition was handed in, signed by twenty-one of the twenty-eight girls, protesting at the system. Despite all this and the in-depth discussion held at the next meeting of the organisers, the method was declared to be fair and would continue to be used unless anything better could be found; they hoped the judging would improve!

The winner of the 1953 contest, Brenda Mee, receives the rather close attention of judges, comedians Abbott and Costello. Lou Costello was renowned for his rather wild behaviour and, while staying at the Midland Hotel for this contest, managed to get locked out while sampling Morecambe's nightlife and was heard in the early hours begging to be let back in!

A contestant maintains a smiling demeanour for the crowd despite the discomforting scrutiny of members of the judging panel.

But who did the judges actually choose? Did any one particular type of young woman repeatedly walk away with the prize?

The winners in the Super Swimming Stadium were in the age range 18-24 with, in the early years, a tendency towards the lower end of that age bracket. Most were slightly above average height for those days (5ft 6in–5ft 7in / 167–170cm), often boosted by their high-heeled footwear. Girls supplied their own personal measurements which were then verified along with checking for any artificial aids to costumes before an appearance. These 'vital statistics' were printed in the programme from 1953 onwards (prior to that, 'salient facts' recorded things like height and hair colour). A trim, symmetrical hour-glass type figure was the preferred choice, waists generally around 23–24 inches (58–61cm) and hips and busts not exceeding 37 inches (94cm). Organisers and contestants alike clung stubbornly to imperial measurements as, in a brief experiment to move with the times, the girls were horrified to find the coveted 36–24–36 figure transformed to 91–61–91 when metricated!

Did gentlemen actually prefer blondes?

Certainly not in the early days when, in general, there was a favourable trend towards brunettes. Contestants gave their own descriptions of hair colour, all perfectly natural in the early days, such as fair, brown, light brown, etc, but later, influenced by the increasing use of hair colourants, rather more fanciful labels (taken directly from the wording on the packet) of silver blonde, mahogany and raven appeared, along with the occasional indignant 'natural blonde'.

Could the choice of swimsuit influence the outcome?

Obviously there was to be no help from padding or boning and in the early days any hint of too great an exposure of cleavage was delicately covered by the use of lace handkerchiefs or artificial flowers. Some swimsuits were definitely more flattering than others. Immediately post-war there was a huge variety of fashions on display – pre-war styles, knitted woollen costumes, ruched ones, shiny, satiny affairs, ones with skirts, two-pieces with bottoms definitely not of the bikini type, patterned and plain, shop bought and home-made. Lydia Reid's success

Competitors line up for a heat at the Super Swimming Stadium in July 1946. Note the multiple swimsuit styles, along with the range of footwear.

in the first final in her plain white one-piece, did, however, seem to spark a trend. In 1946 June Rivers swapped her dark costume of 1945 for a white one and duly won the title. From then on through the 1950s, with very few exceptions, it was the 'woman in white' who took the top prize. The mid-1960s brought a change, with a penchant for plain bright colours prevailing. Gradually the swimsuits got skimpier with cut-out sections revealing large expanses of evenly tanned torsos and, in the 1970s, the rule banning bikinis was eventually relaxed. In the beginning the competitors appear to have accessorised their swimwear with whatever shoes they had arrived in but it was not long before the white stiletto, like the white swimsuit, became the norm. (At one point in the early 1970s shoes were briefly abandoned altogether for the swimwear parade.)

The successful contestant had to be able to maintain her poise and smile while teetering around the pool edge in said high heels and fulfilling the demands of photographers to pose on high diving boards while holding the trophy aloft. She also needed a strong constitution as, despite the offer of the Winter Gardens to host the event in case of inclement weather, this never seemed to happen and the Grand Final took place in the Super Swimming Stadium (while it existed) in all types of British summer weather. There was little relief behind the scenes as the changing rooms were always said to be cold, though perhaps not as cold as the pool in which the beauties were never actually required to bathe.

In this 1952 heat, the top three can be seen in the almost obligatory white costume while, in their white high heels, they tower over the diminutive comedian Arthur Askey, failing to make any impression, with his legs, on them or fellow judge Eddie Gray.

Thousands packed the stadium, vying to take the coveted poolside seats. The competitors paraded within touching distance, trying to turn a deaf ear to the public's comments.

The last sixteen in the 1968 final line up on the diving tower. Most smile and wave confidently to the on-lookers while keeping a firm grip on the handrail. All continue to wear one-piece swimsuits but the new 'cut-away' style reveals considerably more flesh than had been permitted in earlier years.

SWIMSUITS, SUNTANS AND SMILES

The experiences of four young women who took part in the contest at the height of its popularity at the Super Swimming Stadium may shed a little light on the world of the beauty queen. Three were local to Morecambe – **June Dobson**, finalist in 1949, 1951 and again in 1953 under her married name of Wray, **Sheila McGaffigan** in 1957 and 1958, and **Sharman Bardsley** in 1968. The fourth, **Gillian Taylor** from Stockport, carried off the Miss Great Britain title on her third appearance in 1963.

June entered the penultimate heat in August 1949 at the last minute "on a whim, for a bit of fun", with just the experience of an attempt at Miss Morecambe the previous year behind her. She had no great fear of parading before huge crowds as she was used to appearing on stage as a singer and dancer at Morecambe theatres and had taken the lead in a number of amateur productions; she was shortly to achieve her ambition of a professional career on the stage.

As a child Sheila suffered from an illness which badly affected her feet and legs and, after corrective surgery, her doctors suggested that in order to assist recovery, she take up dancing. This not only helped physically but equipped Sheila with poise and confidence, which led to modelling jobs for local businesses. Working in the office of her father's blacksmiths in Bolton-le-Sands brought her into contact with members of the farming community and she was soon being invited to country shows and encouraged to enter their beauty contests. From the age of seventeen when she won second prize at the 'Milk Kitters' Ball' in Morecambe's Floral Hall, Sheila found success on the local circuit, picking up titles such as Dairy Princess, Miss Lunesdale, Kendal Festival Queen and earning herself the soubriquet 'the Belle of Bolton-le-Sands' from the *Visitor*. From there it was a relatively small step to don a swimsuit and try her luck at the Super Swimming Stadium.

Long before Gillian had any thoughts of beauty contests, Morecambe had been a holiday destination with her parents where she had enjoyed swimming in the stadium and watching the Aqua Shows. Later, in order to help build Gillian's confidence and overcome her shyness, her mother enrolled her on a Lucy Clayton 'charm course'. This led to part-time modelling work and success in the Miss Camay competition. Mixing with other like-minded

June Dobson as she appeared at the age of eighteen in her eye-catching borrowed swimsuit. Merely hoping for a small cash prize, she was genuinely surprised to win the heat although she thought the judge, Vera Lynn, may have felt some empathy with her as a fellow singer. Vera reportedly told the crowd that June had been selected from the record entry of 39 hopefuls because of "her deportment and charm as well as her pretty face and figure". June's third appearance in the Grand Final was in 1953 when she had also been chosen as Morecambe's Coronation Queen. She was a beauty whose bathing suit definitely got wet when she joined the Aqua Shows at the Super Swimming Stadium.

While not under any contract to do so at the time, many Miss GB contestants were often asked to appear in publicity photographs to advertise the delights of Morecambe as a holiday resort. Here, in one such shot, Sheila McGaffigan (second right) poses alongside some of her 'friendly rivals' from the local beauty circuit.

young women in the Manchester/Cheshire region encouraged her to enter and win various competitions such as Miss Cheshire Rose, eventually taking her to Morecambe and the Miss GB final.

Sharman's first foray onto the beauty scene was at the age of sixteen, when her father entered her into a photographic contest to be Morecambe's Carnival Queen. Encouraged by taking a runner's-up spot, she tried again the following year and won. Her training as a dancer, with appearances at local theatres and shows at Pontins holiday camp (where she had been one of the youngest Bluecoats) meant that a swimsuit parade before an audience did not faze her – "not that different from performing in a leotard" – and,

following a suggestion from her mother, entered the Miss Morecambe contest at the Super Swimming Stadium. Winning this gave direct entry to the Miss GB final.

Once entered in the contest, there was the problem of what to wear. Despite Eric Morley's assertion (when defending the idea of beauty contests) that it was democratic to assess girls in swimwear as "it is a garment they can all afford", many experienced difficulty in finding that perfect costume which flattered their figure while adhering to the rules and which would catch the judges' eye without breaking the bank. When June entered her heat in 1949, she wore a swimsuit borrowed from a friend who had

Sharman Bardsley (bottom right) and the rest of the 1968 finalists on the staircase of the Midland Hotel, raise a glass to the winner Yvonne Ormes (back to camera). As the second youngest in the final, Sharman had become friendly with the very youngest, a 17-year old who, as well as winning her heat in Morecambe, also held the Miss Wales title. Together they felt rather unsophisticated and in awe of the more 'professional beauties' – many of whom, in actual fact, were not much older.

recently brought it back from the USA. Although Sheila tried to save as much as she could from her prize money, she admitted that a reasonable amount had to be spent on swimsuits, many of them specially made as it was awkward to find ones to fit. In her turn, Sharman was overjoyed to receive a new costume as part of her prize for winning Miss Morecambe – it would have been expensive to replace the one worn in that heat, which only just passed the Miss Fisher inspection with the aid of a strategically placed artificial rose.

Make-up in the early days was minimal – perhaps a dab of lipstick or the sweep of an eyebrow pencil.

A healthy glow was acquired naturally by time spent in the sun. By the time June was making her second appearance in the final she had a new job which gave her good reason for the 'natural look'. The *Visitor* described her as: "An Aquabelle who, only a few minutes before competing, had been swimming in the show. She looked lovely in a turquoise costume."

By the late 1950s a tan was deemed necessary but difficult to acquire without the aid of the artificial agents used nowadays. Sheila remembers everyone with pale skin applying gravy browning to their bodies which, coupled with the use of sugar water to fix their hair, gave a certain aroma to the dressing rooms. Ten years later, according to Sharman, it was "all big hair, fake tans and false eyelashes" – the smell in the changing rooms now redolent of chemical tanning agents and hair lacquer. Sharman had learned to apply make-up in a professional manner to make an impact in her stage work as a dancer and felt that she gained some advantage from that.

Generally, those coming to the contest in the 1950s and 1960s from outside the Morecambe area had the benefit of staying together for a week beforehand, exchanging tips and expertise in use of cosmetics. Their preparations could be more thorough and less hurried than those of the local girls with just the day (or afternoon) off from their everyday jobs. Interestingly, no truly local contestant won the title after Lydia Reid in 1945.

The atmosphere generated by the huge crowds inside the imposing stadium venue had an effect on even the most confident of contestants. Sheila admitted to a slight shiver on stepping out into the giant space, not merely caused by the chilly surroundings while Sharman declared it to be "really, really exciting – like the opening of a show". After her first appearance, Gillian found herself buoyed up by the experience and wanted to return and win. She felt it was necessary to get the crowd on her side and so worked on projecting a warm happy personality as she took the lonely trek around the pool.

Recently married dental nurse and part-time model, Gillian Taylor, in 1963, wearing the embroidered sash bearing the Morecambe and Heysham crest and name. Along with her silver rose bowl, Gillian still has this among mementos of her time as Miss GB. Her rewards for beating 40 other contestants that day included a cheque for £1,000 and a holiday in Italy.

All four had pleasant memories of their Miss GB experience, expressing none of the regrets of some later contestants. They felt that they had known how to look after themselves, that Miss Fisher in her turn had tried to ensure they were looked after and that unwanted attention or exploitation was easily brushed aside. June kept her connection with the stadium by becoming part of the entertainments team, singing and swimming in the Aqua Shows for many summers. Sheila continued to find success in competitions in the region and beyond – one earning her a chance to travel to the USA – and to save enough to buy a house. Still running the office for the family business she continued her part-time modelling career, including the task of wearing an 'unsinkable' swimsuit and, at one such job, meeting her future husband. Sharman and her family struck up an acquaintance with Max Bygraves, one of the judges at the 1968 final, who offered her a job in his son's show in Bournemouth. Preferring a little more independence and to further her ambition to travel, Sharman declined the offer and auditioned instead to work with a dance company in Italy, flying out to Rome at the age of nineteen to tour the country for a year. On her return to the UK she became a dance teacher, eventually opening her own dance school. Although she entered no more beauty competitions, she helped in later years when the Miss Morecambe contest was revived.

For Gillian her win in 1963 was the apex of her beauty career. After stepping down from the podium

Gillian Taylor in her role as ambassadress in the midst of her travels in Glasgow airport. A chance encounter with another beauty queen (Miss Indiana from the USA) gave rise to this photo opportunity. One of Gillian's biggest trips was to Dusseldorf in West Germany to help promote British Industry; she spent most of the time modelling swimsuits and signing photographs. She was also 'adopted' by the King's Own Border Regiment and invited as guest of honour to their regimental dinner.

she declared: "Now I have won the only competition I ever wanted to win … after this, I shall retire from the beauty business." The following year was spent travelling in her role as an ambassadress for Morecambe and the competition, starting almost immediately with her round Britain flight tour. Gillian opened fêtes, gave out prizes, modelled clothing, made TV appearances – always endeavouring to live up to the expectations of Miss Fisher and Morecambe and Heysham Corporation to remain permanently pleasant and well-mannered. On her longer trips she was usually accompanied by Miss Fisher who made all the arrangements and the two developed a friendship which lasted for the remainder of Dorothy Fisher's life. Gillian stayed in contact with many other winners of the Miss GB title and was chosen to make a presentation on their behalf on Miss Fisher's retirement.

THE REAL MISS GREAT BRITAIN

The one person who truly deserves the title 'Miss Great Britain' is **Miss Dorothy Fisher**.

Born in Preston and having spent some of her early life in Workington, Dorothy came to Lancaster in 1937 to take the job of secretary to the overseas manager of Williamson's linoleum company. She was the first woman to join the local Home Guard, working in its Lancaster office during World War Two. In 1945 she moved to Morecambe Town Hall and shortly after the war's end, found herself running the Publicity Department almost single-handedly and becoming involved with the victory celebrations in the town. The National Bathing Beauty Competition, initiated as part of these festivities, became her personal project for the next twenty-nine years.

According to the *Visitor*: 'Every Wednesday this five foot of efficiency can be seen checking and re-checking to ensure that nothing goes wrong with the organisation. Each year, after the final, three or four weeks pass and Miss Fisher is at it again, making preparations for the following year's contest.' Miss Fisher herself described her duties as "pleasurable but hard work".

Her efforts were rewarded with invitations each year to accompany the new Miss GB on trips both home and abroad. Despite never being off duty on these occasions, Dorothy was able to indulge her love of travel to a number of exotic locations in Europe, Asia, Africa and North America; travel ranged from planes and luxury cruise liners to the more unusual, if slightly less comfortable, camel (a desert excursion in Tunisia). Acting as chaperone to Miss GB, Dorothy Fisher often shared the limelight and VIP treatment at shows, festivals, studios and embassies, unfazed by her meetings with captains of industry, royalty and stars of stage and screen.

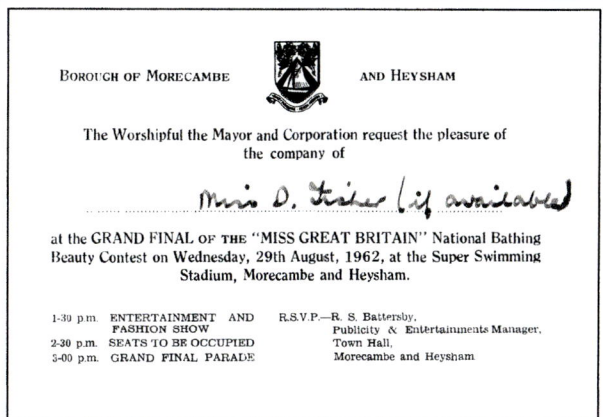

A rather strange notion that Miss Fisher needed an invitation to the final of a Miss GB contest – without her, the whole event would have proved impossible to stage.

Dorothy Fisher at work in Morecambe's Publicity Department. On her retirement in 1973 she was presented with a picnic hamper and declared that she intended to travel and write a book based on her experiences. She had a large collection of souvenirs of her time with Miss GB, photographs and letters, often addressed to 'Dear Aunty' from former contestants and their families. (After her death these were bequeathed to Gillian Taylor who, in turn, kindly donated the majority to the archives of Morecambe Heritage Centre.)

As a reward for her twenty-nine years' service, Dorothy was given the privilege of choosing the judges for her last Miss GB final in 1973. Her choice fell on five former winners with whom she felt a particular rapport. She is seen here with (front left to right) Gillian Taylor 1963, Christina Mayo 1958, (back left to right) Brenda Mee 1953, Jennifer Gurley 1967, Gay Spink, newly crowned 1973 Miss GB and Elizabeth Robinson 1972.

She elicited mixed feelings among the bathing beauties; many waited in trepidation for the lists of instructions to keep the proceedings flowing and the inspections to ensure strict adherence to costume rules – Miss Fisher was reputed to have a very sharp eye for 'falsies', artificial support and too much exposure. At the same time she was very much appreciated for the concern she showed for the girls in her charge and her encouragement of those of a nervous disposition. In particular, Dorothy developed warm friendships with many of the title winners who she accompanied on their travels, providing a reassuring presence for the young women in strange locations away from friends and family. The verdict of the contestants was summed up by Gillian Taylor (Miss GB 1963), who presented her with a cut-glass rose bowl on their behalf after the 1973 final. "Dorothy has been with the competition right from the word go and she has not stopped for one moment looking after the girls and attending to their every need. She has been a father confessor, mother and nursemaid to us all."

Post-retirement, Dorothy fulfilled her aim to travel, often using the opportunity to accept invitations to visit former contestants. Here she is seen with film star Anne Heywood (the former Violet Pretty) on Lake Geneva.

SEVEN

Following the appearance of a leak in the Super Swimming Stadium and the postponement of its opening for the 1974 season, rumours began to circulate that its condition was so bad that it might have to be demolished. While the shabbiness of the terraces, rotting steps, peeling paintwork and cracks in the render were plain to see, the main problems lay in the sub-structure below pool level hidden from public view. Steel supports had corroded badly and needed additional strengthening while in places concrete had cracked and crumbled, leading to accusations that Morecambe Corporation had been negligent in its maintenance of the building, accusations which were vigorously refuted. Some blamed the stadium's deterioration on the use of sub-standard concrete in its construction while others pointed to its seafront location and nearly forty years exposure to salt-laden winds and rain. Whether culpability lay with the contractors, Morecambe Corporation or the elements was by now academic. Decisions had to be made. Minds were focused when Derek Illsley, the Borough Engineer, after a detailed inspection, found the building to be in a much worse state than he had previously thought and concluded that "something over £100,000 would be needed to bring the stadium up to scratch".

Structural defects had first been identified two years earlier and in 1973 concerns for the safety of bathers and spectators had resulted in sections of the terracing being cordoned off although the pool itself remained open for use throughout the summer. Around this time plans for a new Sports Complex/Leisure Centre were being considered for a site on Morecambe Road. Difficulties in purchasing the land had cropped up, however, leading to the possibility of switching location to Morecambe's seafront in place of the ageing swimming stadium. In the opinion of the then Town Clerk, Charles Bottomley, if the project were to go ahead the town would gain an attraction much more valuable even than the Super Swimming Stadium. He did not regard the stadium as being beyond redemption but said: "If one were to repair it then one would have to find another site for the complex. It's not so much a matter of losing the stadium but gaining the Sports Complex/Leisure Centre."

By June 1974 it was looking increasingly likely that the swimming stadium would be demolished although not everyone was persuaded. Opponents included a number of Conservatives on the newly created Lancaster City Council. One of these was the mayor, Councillor John Elliot, who pressed the Chief Executive, Donald Waddell, for a meeting to ascertain if the stadium could be repaired and opened later in the season. Waddell was sceptical, believing it to be "beyond redemption" but was willing to wait for an opinion from the original contractors before recommending a course of action.

In the meantime civil engineers investigating the problem had discovered the existence of not just one leak but several. After a fortnight's remedial work, during which the leaks were sealed, the pool was filled with water. As tests revealed no evidence of any seepage the Council decided to reopen the stadium on July 13th for an abbreviated season. Allan Heppenstall, the Council's Planner/Architect, warned: "It must be clearly understood that the work carried out is merely a patching exercise and it must not be assumed that the pool can either remain open for the rest of the season or will be available thereafter."

Later that month the building was visited by Dennis Weiner, chairman of the contractors Sir Lindsay Parkinson & Sons Ltd. He was not surprised at its condition. "Bearing in mind the exposed situation, this is not unexpected after forty years." He counselled against trying to repair the damage. "As I understand it, the present situation does not of itself prove a sound economic proposition. It therefore seems to me that it would be preferable to build a new swimming pool to Olympic standards under cover, with a considerable area on the south side for sunbathing." In the light of this appraisal the Council decided to commission a structural survey of the stadium's condition from consulting engineers Felix J. Samuely and Partners of London.

In October, at a meeting of the Council's Economic Development Committee regarding the Super Swimming Stadium, Charles Bottomley, now Tourist Development Officer, said the season had been a catastrophe and wanted to know whether the stadium would open in 1975. The likelihood of this happening was remote, according to Allan Heppenstall, who told the Committee that the shallow end of the pool was in danger of collapse. Another ominous crack had developed in the structure and if the stadium opened for swimming next year there was a 50-50 chance of a major disaster. He admitted he did not like going inside the building and that its staff were "very edgy". The Committee agreed to await the structural engineer's report before finally condemning the stadium but, fearing the worst, considered it would be unwise to include it in Morecambe's 1975 Holiday Guide.

Felix J. Samuely and Partners' report was blunt. They concluded that the building was in such a poor/dangerous state that they had no alternative but to advise that it be closed to the public. "In the circumstances we cannot envisage (nor therefore recommend) any temporary repair work which could make the pool safe for even a short period other than a completely new construction on proper foundations." The Council felt it was left with no option other than to recommend the immediate closure of the stadium on safety grounds, a decision made easier by its insurers withdrawing cover for the building. However, an influential group of Conservative councillors argued that the stadium's problems had been exaggerated and believed it was being used as a "sort of 'sacrificial cow' on the altar of a sport and leisure centre". They wanted to see the stadium retained and called for a more in-depth examination to find out what it would cost to repair and by how long its life could be extended as a result.

Crumbling concrete is obvious on the terracing adjacent to the stadium café.

Timber props were needed to provide additional support for the terraces.

This was provided by the same consultants in August 1975 and included reasons why, in their view, the stadium should be condemned. "The concrete members of the terraces were in such a condition that, except for a thin outer skin to the beams, the cement was almost non-existent. In the settling tank area timber props had been inserted in an attempt to retain the terrace above. Beams, columns and slabs had deteriorated to such an extent that the concrete was disintegrating and exposed reinforcement severely corroded. The side walls to the pool were also showing the same signs of deterioration and at one point of the shallow end water was seeping through the concrete above the water line in the pool." They were convinced that to allow the public to use the stadium would be dangerous, as any failure due to the condition of the structural members would be sudden and, in the worst case, lead to loss of life. Even this damning assessment failed to convince a hard core of Conservatives. John Elliot claimed he had been assured by a consultant engineer he knew that the stadium could be repaired for £100,000 and if it cost any more he was prepared to pay the difference himself! They requested another firm investigate.

In September, Oxfordshire based structural engineer J.M. Plowman considered the effects of the stadium's location on its deterioration. "The whole site is completely exposed to winds blowing across Morecambe Bay and the sea comes within a few feet of the sea wall at every high tide. It may be assumed that every part of the concrete structure had been surrounded by air of high humidity and very high salts content throughout the whole of its life and that the upper parts have been frequently washed by spume driven by the wind. I formally recommend that the pool, surrounds and bridges be declared DANGEROUS STRUCTURES." He concluded that the deterioration was of such a degree that it would be uneconomic to attempt to repair any part of the complex.

Although three separate surveys had been carried out by specialist structural engineers and all had reached the same conclusion – namely that any attempt at repairing the stadium would not be economically viable – this still did not satisfy certain councillors. Seemingly unconcerned about spending even more taxpayers' money on a lost cause, they called a special meeting to ask yet another firm for its opinion. By now the number of meetings convened to discuss the future of the stadium was well into double figures and rising.

It came as little surprise when the verdict of White, Young and Partners, Consulting Civil and Structural Engineers of Lytham St. Annes, delivered in February 1976, endorsed previous advice to close the building. Their investigation had found poorly compacted concrete with high levels of calcium chloride and inadequate cover of steel reinforcements which had resulted in serious corrosion of the metal. They had particular concern for the covered ways at either end of the pool, the settling tanks, the filter room and the terraces over them. The most difficult part of any potential restoration would be those areas below high-water level including the foundations and pool wall. Their summary was brief and to the point. "In our view, the extent of reconstruction that is required does not prove repairs to be an economic proposition."

This appeared to end the debate and in early March a resolution was passed by 27 votes to 20 to demolish the stadium and build a new pool and leisure park at a cost of £985,000. One councillor said he would be sad to see the old stadium knocked down but conceded that "a new Mini that goes is better than a clapped-out Rolls Royce". Following this decision an application signed by sixteen councillors for another special meeting to discuss the stadium's future was granted, to the exasperation of the new mayor, Councillor Janet Horner. "Top consultants in the country have said it is not a viable proposition and we are turning round and telling them we don't believe them. If we cannot take the advice and the recommendations of consultants we have engaged in time we will get no consultants willing to come forward and do anything for us. Had the project we passed not been delayed, we would have been well on our way to having a new pool." It was now clear that divisions between the two main political parties on the City Council had hardened. While the Labour group was solidly in favour of a replacement, most Conservatives wanted to retain the stadium although, as a cartoon in the *Morecambe Guardian* intimated, a few needed encouraging to toe the party line.

Opinions were also divided outside the political arena. At a meeting of the executive committee of the Morecambe and Heysham Chamber of Trade in April, Mr R. Lancaster argued that if York Minster can be repaired so could Morecambe's Super Swimming Stadium, adding that the proposed replacement pool would be more like "a duck pond" in comparison. "To pull down the stadium would be to destroy part of Morecambe", he said. Mr G. Nicholson, on the other hand, described the stadium as "Morecambe's Colosseum" and declared: "It wants pulling down. The day when people came in their thousands to walk along the piers chatting to each other had gone and it was the same with the stadium."

A reconfiguration of Lancaster City Council following local elections in May added more Conservatives to the campaign to keep the stadium, resulting in a vote to suspend demolition pending further investigations to see if any part of it was capable of repair and, if so, what it would cost. J.M. Plowman, who had produced a report the previous September, was contacted for his opinion by Donald Waddell and did not mince his words. "Much of my practice consists of testing structures. In the case of your pool complex I am quite convinced that any further testing of what is already known would needlessly waste much time and money." Ignoring his advice, councillors voted to needlessly waste much time and money and approved two more surveys, a decision criticised by Labour as the result of "misguided fanatical enthusiasm".

"It wasn't until the party boss told me 'vote for the tests or else' that I realised what a wonderful architectural gem our Swimming Stadium is."

On 14th July, at yet another meeting (now exceeding forty), Donald Waddell reported that the latest surveys had indicated that in order to extend the stadium's life Lancaster City Council could be faced with a bill of between £500,000 and £600,000. He added that these were accurate figures and not assumptions. Council leader George Walling stressed the need for a quick decision, worried that Morecambe might end up with no swimming pool facilities which would be disastrous for the resort. Despite his plea for a once-and-for-all resolution, a motion was passed to find out how much it would cost for the stadium to be redesigned, perhaps by reducing the size of the pool by a third, making the water shallower and demolishing all the structure apart from the front of the building. One Labour councillor dismissed the scheme as "a mixed-up abortion" while another said: "At the end of the day you would have a patched-up job which could almost symbolise a patched-up resort."

It was pointed out that back in March, when the previous Council had voted in favour of a new pool, the County Allocation Committee had given its permission for Lancaster City Council to borrow the £985,000 on the basis of a timetable which provided for a physical start to the project by the end of the year. Time was running out and if a decision on the future of the stadium was not made soon the money could be in jeopardy. Crucially, because repairs to the existing pool could not be financed under the allocation scheme, payment for them would have to come out of the rates.

The Council's next meeting lasted over five hours and still failed to reach a decision. After several heated and often acrimonious exchanges between the two political parties, the mayor, now Councillor Peter Sumner, was forced to bring it to an end "to preserve sanity", by which time only 40 of the original 59 councillors still remained. A follow-up meeting was hurriedly arranged prior to which councillors were warned by angry hoteliers to make a final decision or get out, claiming they had lost the confidence of the electorate. One said: "It's like the *Forsyte Saga*, it's going on forever!" They proposed writing to the Prime Minister to order councillors to pay back expenses received for attendance at, in their view, an unnecessary plethora of meetings.

Finally, a decision! After two and a half years of wrangling, on September 12th, at the forty-seventh meeting in which the future of the Super Swimming Stadium had been debated at Committee and Council level, a motion to demolish the stadium and build a heated outdoor pool on the site was passed by 34 votes to 19. Several Conservatives who had originally supported the campaign to retain the building changed their minds and voted in favour of the motion.

In October the Council accepted a tender of £88,867 from Harbour and General (the lowest of five received) for the demolition of the stadium. The work was estimated to take three months including filling in and levelling of the site. At the beginning of November the bulldozers moved in and by the following Easter no trace of Morecambe's Super Swimming Stadium remained.

BATHS SUPERINTENDENTS

Over the four decades of its existence the Super Swimming Stadium had only four Baths Superintendents/Managers.

| Leonard Flook | 1936-1947 | Norman Walker | 1948-1949 |
| George Campbell Cooper | 1950-1965 | Glynn D. Smith | 1966-1976 |

(Edward Pinder was temporarily in charge for parts of 1964 and 1965)

By December 1976 both curved ends of the stadium and some of the terracing had been demolished and much of the rubble removed.

While the demolition of the Super Swimming Stadium was mourned by many, in the context of the time its demise was not entirely unexpected. By the 1970s most outdoor swimming pools in Britain were struggling to survive, only managing to keep open thanks to large subsidies from their local councils. Like Morecambe's stadium those lidos built in the 1920s and 1930s were facing mounting problems. Physical deterioration from decades of exposure to salt-laden winds and rain, lack of maintenance due to local authority cutbacks, new health and safety regulations and rising insurance premiums were all combining to make the continued existence of such pools financially unviable.

As purse strings were further tightened in the 1980s, councils could no longer afford to bail out their local pools and they began to close. In North-West England the axe fell on Blackpool's Open Air Baths in 1983 followed by Southport's Sea Bathing Lake in 1989. Falling attendances prompted the closure of New Brighton's vast pool a year later. The small lido at Grange-over-Sands hung on until 1993 but eventually succumbed (although there are plans for its renovation and reopening).

Given all the evidence that outdoor swimming pools lose money, how then would Morecambe respond to the closure of its Super Swimming Stadium? The answer: it would build a new outdoor swimming pool.

GREAT EXPECTATIONS AND HARD TIMES

EIGHT

Following the decision to demolish the Super Swimming Stadium, the plans for its replacement were passed by Lancaster City Council with little dissent. Not only would there be a new pool but a whole new Leisure Park, with a price tag of £4 million. Building of the first phase, the pool, was scheduled to begin in May 1977 and be completed for the 1978 season.

When it was discovered that the pool would not be covered the news was greeted with disbelief. What was the point of another outdoor pool, even if it was to be heated, when it could be open for just a few months in summer and was almost certain to lose money? A 'Roof the Pool' campaign developed over the following weeks with suggestions including a roof which could retract, allowing full enclosure in poor weather but be open to the sun in summer. Feelings ran high, culminating in a protest march and the handing in of a 15,000 signature petition. In response, the Council explained that a roof required much stronger foundations at substantial extra cost and would push the target date for completion 'out of the window'. In early 1977 the simple truth was acknowledged – there was no more money in the kitty for any type of cover for the new pool.

Anxiety was also expressed about the length of time Morecambe would be without safe swimming facilities. It had already been two years since the Super Swimming Stadium closed and there would be at least a further two years to wait. This the Council addressed by promising that the smaller indoor pools provided at Carnforth, Hornby and Heysham High Schools would be available for use by the public outside school hours.

Morecambe was not alone in its struggle to finance new projects. The 1970s witnessed the rapid decline of traditional heavy industry leading to widespread unemployment and industrial unrest. World-wide shortages of oil coupled with miners' strikes devastated power supplies and pushed up the cost of transport (along with everything else). Serious inflation ensued and the pound fell in value; the cost of living rose dramatically while wages were kept steady by imposing pay freezes – few in old industrial Lancashire and Yorkshire had money to spare.

This, of course, had a knock-on effect on the health of Morecambe as a seaside resort. No industry meant no 'wakes weeks' and no packed excursion trains leaving the mill towns of West Yorkshire and South Lancashire, disgorging their thousands seeking the simple pleasures of a week of fresh air and fun. Those lucky enough to have money usually owned a car, meaning that almost anywhere in Britain was within relatively easy reach. Morecambe's traditional clientele began to turn their sights elsewhere – Devon and Cornwall rose in popularity. Even more popular was the prospect of a holiday with almost guaranteed sunshine and accommodation in a modern hotel away from Britain's grey seas, cardigans and plastic macs. Cheaper flights and package deals meant that it was possible to have a week on the Mediterranean coast for a similar price to that of a week in Morecambe in an old-fashioned boarding house presided over by a fearsome landlady with strict rules about mealtimes and shared bathrooms. In a survey of twenty-six holiday destinations carried out by the *Visitor* at that time, the two most popular were Majorca and Benidorm while Morecambe languished at number twenty-five with only Clacton in Essex less favoured. Morecambe became the type of place visited for half a day at the weekend or where pensioners on coach tours stayed cheaply in the chilly days before or after 'the season'.

Tastes in holiday activities were changing too. People were no longer content just to sit on the beach (especially a damp and windy one) or stroll along the pier and spend their loose change in slot machines. There was a growing interest in the countryside and visits to historical and cultural attractions. Morecambe's close neighbour, Lancaster, could provide theatres, cinemas, museums, a castle (even though visits were restricted by its prison status) and many gems of Georgian architecture. Nearby villages such as Arnside, Silverdale and Kirkby Lonsdale were suitably picturesque and the Lake District, viewed clearly across the bay, was within easy reach by car so that even those choosing to stay in Morecambe could be enticed away to spend their money elsewhere. The resort was often relegated to an afterthought in the local holiday guide.

After its amalgamation with Lancaster in 1974, Morecambe developed a serious case of jealousy of its neighbour; the town felt it was being starved of money while the city prospered. Lancaster was blamed for Morecambe's decline. The truth is that the decline had set in much earlier. While some seaside resorts had moved with the times aiming to attract a younger, better off clientele, Morecambe slid, seemingly oblivious, into the 1960s, relying on its traditional trade. Investment in new attractions (or even upkeep of old favourites) was virtually non-existent. The physical fabric of the town had become shabby and run down. Tired accommodation failed to be up-dated and was slow to adapt to more flexible lengths of stay. Morecambe was a disaster waiting to happen and the 1970s duly obliged.

On one hot summer's day in 1970, fire completely destroyed the faux pirate ship Moby Dick and devastated the Alhambra theatre. By 1973 parts of the Super Swimming Stadium were in such poor condition they had to be closed to the public. Two years later Central Pier was so damaged that it too had to shut for a time and in early 1977 gales completely destroyed West End Pier. That same year Morecambe's biggest theatre, the Winter Gardens, brought its curtain down for the last time having consistently lost money during the previous decade. The fact that so many disused cinemas and theatres in the town became venues for the increasingly popular pastime of bingo earned it the disparaging title of 'Bingoville by the Sea'. Following Dr Beeching's axe, mainline rail services no longer reached Morecambe (merely becoming the end of a local service from Lancaster) and Euston Road station closed. The comedian Colin Crompton summed up the situation when he made Morecambe the butt of his jokes, describing it as the 'Costa Geriatrica' and 'the place where people went to die but forgot why they went'.

This plan, printed in the *Visitor* in August 1978, attempted to inform the public of what the new Leisure Park would be like when completed.

Phase 1
A   Heated open-air pool with wave machine, swimming lanes and banked spectator terracing
B   Children's paddling pool and play area
C   Changing rooms at pool level and café above
D   Entrance
E   Aeration and splash pool
F   Pumphouse
G   Partition separating Leisure Park from promenade

Phase 2
H   Covered area (still at pre-design stage)
I   Toilets and storage area
J   Arena with sales kiosks
K   New entrance to Harbour Band Arena

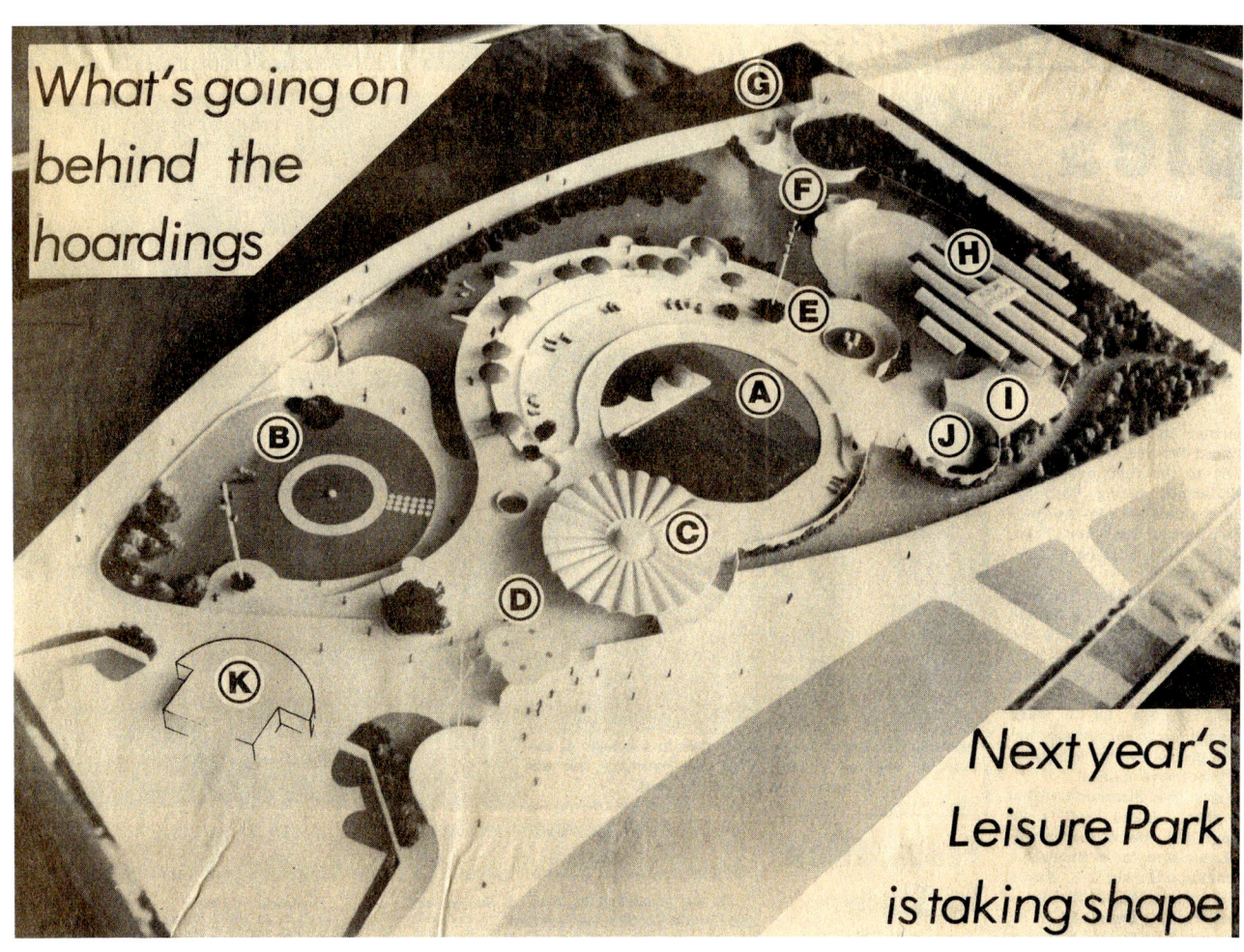

This then was the climate in which Morecambe's new pool took shape. Construction began in late June 1977, more than a month later than originally intended, the contract having been awarded to the Preston firm of John Turner and Sons. Costs had risen by 25% because of extra drainage needed on the site and the date for completion was now expected to be December 1978 ready for opening at Easter 1979. Good news arrived in the summer of 1978 in the form of a large grant from the EEC which would enable the provision of some longed-for covered accommodation in the second phase of the Leisure Park development. Plans for this were immediately put in place in the expectation that this project (put out to separate tender) would be ready for use in 1980.

Easter 1979 came and went with no sign of the Leisure Park being ready but eventually, in May, the pool was filled with water and the public was invited to a preview before the official opening on June 20th. The *Lancashire Evening Post* reported on a new optimism in Morecambe, describing the complex as 'the most significant contribution to the well-being of this resort for many years'. Unlike the grand opening of its predecessor, the Super Swimming Stadium in 1936, that of the Leisure Park was a much simpler affair. The mayor, Councillor Ivy Welldrake, with a small group of councillors and tourism officials, attempted to enter. She fed her 60p into the ticket machine which promptly

The Blue Lagoon and children's paddling pool. When the Leisure Park opened in 1979, 'Fun for all the family' included music, dancing, keep-fit, 5-a-side football, Caribbean and Hawaiian nights, Punch & Judy and, every Wednesday, Miss GB heats.

Heated Pool, Paddling Pool, Wave Machine, Cafeteria, Bars, Picnic Areas, Shop, Sea Views, Sun Bathing.

Shows, Sports and Fabulous Fun for all the family.

For party bookings and further details, contact the Manager: 0524 419419

● **Open daily from 10.00 a.m.**

failed to print correctly, meaning the whole process had to be repeated. As she tried to pass through the turnstile its mechanism jammed, trapping her between the metal bars. She was eventually freed but not before one of the bars had come off in her rescuer's hand. Apart from that, it all went very smoothly!

The first member of the public to enter was 19-year old Derek O'Connor who had queued for just over half an hour to be sure of being in at the start – in 1936 people had queued virtually all day. Nearly 2,500 visited on the opening day, declaring themselves well satisfied with the Blue Lagoon's 75°F (24°C) temperature and the action of the wave machine. The 60p entrance fee was deemed to be good value, allowing access to a host of other activities as well as the swimming pool. One of the first major events was the *Lancashire Evening Post* sponsored Miss Morecambe Bay contest which gave the winner a place in the Miss GB final. Other early entertainments were a Junior Miss GB final compered by Pete Murray (and won by 10-year old Tanya Schipelbaum who earned £200 and a trip to Disneyland) and a standing-on-one-leg competition (won by Willie Dando who ate raw mackerel, eggs and onions while doing so).

A week after the opening the *Visitor* reported a rather defensive City Tourism Director, Tom Flanagan, as saying that the new venture was a leisure pool and should not be compared with the demolished Super Swimming Stadium. "We understand that people will not forget the stadium but our attitude is that we don't want to know … but to get on with it." He was certain that everyone would be as proud of the Leisure Park as they had been of the stadium in the 1930s. By the end of August it was being hailed as a resounding success.

The contract for the second phase had been awarded to the Eden Construction Company of Carlisle who began work on the £768,617 project in July 1979, aiming for completion in mid-1980. A multi-purpose indoor arena and bar covered by a hundred foot PVC 'space-age' dome was to be the main focal point. The venue would be heated to allow its use for a variety of sports, concerts, dancing and shows all year round. Unfortunately, 1980 proved to be one of Morecambe's worst seasons ever – bad weather and serious unemployment cut the number of visitors, leaving the Council desperately short of funds. A major strike delayed the delivery of building materials and the costs for the new Superdome escalated to £900,000. J.D. Waddell, chief executive of Lancaster City Council, suggested that it should be seen as an investment because "a resort authority has to provide certain facilities for the holiday-maker … there are a lot of facilities in a resort where you have to say 'that costs money' but it is all part and parcel of providing something for people to encourage them to come". Encouragement was in short supply when the Superdome finally opened on Wednesday 10th December to a general lack of interest; for the first event, a semi-final of Miss GB, only one third of the 450 tickets were sold. Tom Flanagan expressed his disappointment: "I expected people to be far more enthusiastic about it. I realise they may be fed up of bathing beauty contests but I thought they would have been interested enough to support the first event being held at the Superdome."

The Leisure Park failed to revive Morecambe's fortunes. The pool suffered in the same way as any other outdoor attraction, with attendances dependent on the weather. On

Morecambe & Lancaster

Morecambe Leisure Park and Superdome.

one particularly hot weekend in June 1986 more than 4,000 visitors paid to enter but on another occasion, in what had generally been a poor summer, a passer-by reported seeing only one child having a swim in 'wind-lashed water'. Extensive preparations necessary at the beginning of each season meant there could be no spontaneous openings in the spring/early summer in good weather and there were frequent grumbles about the times of closure in September. There were also problems with materials used in the pool; on one memorable occasion in 1983 bathers emerged from the water bright blue, the result of substantial quantities of paint flaking off the interior of the Blue Lagoon. While not necessarily hazardous, this was seriously unpleasant and caused closure of the pool for tests to be carried out.

The much vaunted Superdome failed to live up to expectations. The 1981 summer shows saw mounting losses leading to a number of cancellations. A major complaint was the discomfort experienced by audiences and performers alike – the material of which it was constructed allowed the building to heat up like a greenhouse in the summer but let the warmth escape in winter, leaving it exceedingly chilly. Fans and heaters were employed, the plastic was painted (unsuccessfully) and even whitewash was suggested. Eventually, in February 1984, it was decided to give the Superdome £67,000 worth of aluminium cladding to cure the excessive temperature fluctuations, despite a warning that this was simply a waste of money.

By the middle of the decade the Council had declared the Leisure Park to be 'a massive drain on resources' and 'an inefficient way of spending ratepayers' money'. Losses were estimated at £200,000 a year, roughly £2.50 per visit, although it was pointed out that the 125,000 who had visited in the last year of poor weather may not have come at all if the park had not been there. Determined to make a go of it, the organisers began a project in early 1985 to install a further attraction, a giant water chute christened the Big Bender. The £150,000 cost would be borne by a private firm who would run it and take the profits. Due to open at the beginning of June, the project suffered the inevitable delay, this time caused by a fire at the Midlands factory producing the chute sections. Sourcing replacements meant it was a month late when the Big Bender came into use.

After yet another disappointing year with the added problems of vandalism and an infestation of rabbits, concern for the future of the complex was growing. Realisation finally began to dawn that the Leisure Park would continue to be a 'white elephant' if its use could not be extended beyond four months out of every year – the pool needed a roof! £15,000 was put aside for a feasibility study and finally, in early 1987, plans were revealed. The overall operation of the Leisure Park was to be transferred to Clifford Barnett Developments of Leeds who were to build a new 'exotic' indoor pool on the site of the children's paddling pool, promising 'lots of fun and action'. The Council would pay a set amount of £525,000 a year for the new Bubbles venture which compared favourably with the projected £750,000 annual debt in the present situation. Work would begin in March 1988 and be completed in time for the 1989 season.

An early 1980s aerial view of the Leisure Park on a summer's day, crowded with visitors. The Superdome is seen with its original problematic roof before the addition of aluminium cladding.

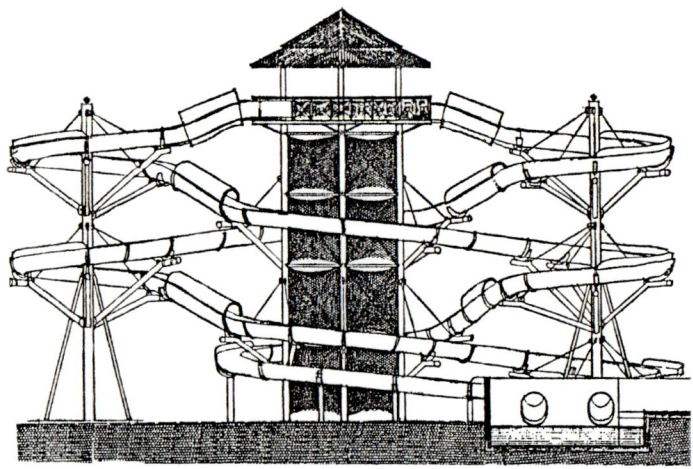

Architect's drawing of the Big Bender. Hailed as 'the biggest and best twin water chute in the land' when it opened in 1985, it stood just over 15 metres high with two chutes, each approximately 50 metres in length. Users climbed to the top of the tower where, supervised by attendants, they were propelled by jets of warm water into a specially made reception pool situated between the Blue Lagoon and the Superdome.

Looking across the Blue Lagoon to the Big Bender and the Superdome with its replacement roof.

View from the top of the Big Bender, over the Blue Lagoon and artificial beach with the Midland Hotel and Harbour Bandstand in the background.

Thus the 1980s ended on an optimistic note with the developers declaring confidence in Morecambe as an area for investment. Lancaster and Morecambe were said to be 'up and coming'; there were good hotels, there was talk of a marina and it was an ideal touring location with the hope of a new road link to the M6. Quite where this optimism came from is hard to imagine. If the 1970s had been bad for Morecambe, in many ways the 1980s were even worse. By 1990 the number of places for holidaymakers to stay had dropped below 200 compared with over 900 in 1960. There were, however, nearly 15,000 bungalows mostly occupied by people of pensionable age and many ex-hotels had been converted into nursing and residential homes for the elderly; Morecambe's population was ageing. For those residents of working age the situation was grim. Wards in Morecambe regularly recorded unemployment rates in excess of 40% and the West End was christened the 'Costa del Dole'. A survey in 1983 made Morecambe out to be 'the cheapest place in Britain'. Advertisements began to appear in Blackburn and Liverpool newspapers, inducing the unemployed there to give up their homes and move to Morecambe, supported by the DHSS. Inner city problems accompanied them into the West End – yet another reason for the tourists to stay away.

The remaining vestiges of the old seaside began to disappear. The Winter Gardens ballroom was demolished in 1982 although the theatre building remained, empty and neglected, its fabric deteriorating. A fire destroyed parts of Central Pier in 1986 and, despite promises of restoration, it too was demolished with much of its ornate ironwork being sold abroad. After the closure of the Palace in 1982 there was no theatre in Morecambe and for a time it was without a cinema. The traditional fairgrounds disappeared to be replaced by the mini theme park, Frontierland (until its demise in 1999). The Illuminations lost their dazzle, always compared unfavourably with those in Blackpool, and fewer and fewer turned up for the switch-on. Morecambe was losing its main purpose, illustrated by the stark decline in revenue from tourism – estimated at £46.6 million in 1973 but only £6.5 million in 1990. It was said 'Morecambe is not yet dead but should be put into intensive care'.

All through these troubled times Morecambe clung on to what had once been its biggest draw – Miss GB. In 1976, having lost its home in the Super Swimming Stadium and then its Winter Gardens venue, the final was held outside Morecambe for the first time – in the Berengaria Theatre of Pontins Holiday Camp at Middleton. Yorkshire TV continued to show scenes of Morecambe in its coverage, keeping the resort's name in the minds of the television audience. Finalists were still drawn from competitions throughout the country as well as the heats held in Morecambe itself. These took place in the Harbour Band Arena adjacent to the old swimming stadium site, to the accompaniment of organist Harold Graham – unless wet, when other venues such as the Central Pier ballroom or the Inn on the Bay were pressed into service.

Arthur Casson remembers becoming compere in 1978, complete with bell-bottom trousers and a new curly perm. "Every Wednesday the girls would assemble while I introduced the panel of judges. I then chatted to each contestant, talking about their home town, day job, hobbies and so on – even about knitting and baking! The girls then paraded around the arena and along the aisles between the rows of deck-chairs. The event moved to the Superdome when it opened and we used the Leisure Park's pool for the parade unless it was full of swimmers. We tried it once when the pool was crowded and the girls complained that they were being splashed and their leg make-up was running! We then held it on the nearby grassed area which was more suitable for photographs."

By now audiences at the heats and even the final were dwindling while the television audiences numbered millions. Lancaster City Council accepted that the contest was no longer an attraction for visitors but its TV coverage still provided valuable publicity for the resort. In 1980 Yorkshire TV pulled out and the BBC took over televising the final. While the heats continued in Morecambe and elsewhere much as before, the final was removed from the district completely and held in London the following January to suit BBC schedules. Film crews recorded earlier stages of the competition and scenes of Morecambe for the Friday night viewing which gave the resort some of its best ever publicity with shots of the sea front, the Leisure Park, the Illuminations, the (short-lived) Big Wheel, power-boat racing and views across the bay. It was estimated to be worth £200,000 of advertising and triggered a rush for the holiday guide. The BBC agreed a contact for the next five years.

After this promising start dissatisfaction soon began to set in; the very next year the Council felt Morecambe had received less than its fair share of publicity. In reply, the show's producer said that his camera crew had driven up and down the promenade for forty-five minutes without finding anything they had not filmed before. There was talk of using other venues such as Leighton Hall and it was even suggested the swimsuit parade could be held in Lancaster's twin town of Perpignan!

By the mid-1980s there was a general feeling that people regarded the contest as a television spectacle and the link to Morecambe was lost despite most of the work involved being carried out in the resort. A survey by the *Morecambe Guardian* after the 1983 final revealed that only a third of the local population supported the contest's continuation while less than 30% thought the television publicity worth the expense, a typical response being 'it's only on TV for old fellas to watch'.

The fall in viewing figures, coupled with an increasingly hostile attitude to the competition among members of the public and the media, caused the BBC in 1985 to announce it was ceasing coverage, despite having another year of its contract to run. The Council's reaction was mixed. Councillor Stanley Henig summed up one side's opinions, describing the contest as "profoundly offensive to some and profoundly boring to all; Miss GB has reached the end of the line". He feared Morecambe would be left to host it because "no-one else wants it". The opposing view, that every seaside resort has a bathing beauty contest and that Morecambe should keep up the tradition, narrowly held sway.

In charge once more, Lancaster City Council, struggling with its finances, managed to raise a little sponsorship and received £8,600 in compensation from the BBC for breach of contract but an extra burden still fell on the ratepayers. Costs were cut to a minimum – the top prize was kept at £4,000 because 'the girls expect it' but there were no fees for judges and therefore no celebrities. Heats, linked with other entertainments to help save revenue, were held in the Superdome as was the final. None of these drew a large audience but as the *Lancashire Evening Post* pointed out: 'Somehow the sombre indoor surroundings of Morecambe's Superdome doesn't lend itself to the competition in the same way that the much lamented open air Swimming Stadium did in those bygone good old days.'

By 1988 the contest was on its last legs. The words, National Bathing Beauty, were dropped from the title and attempts made to scrap the swimwear section completely. Interest was waning even among the competitors – at one heat just two girls turned up to parade before an audience of fewer than a hundred. The final was held in January 1989 away from Morecambe, at the National Exhibition Centre in Birmingham as part of a Travel and Tourism Fair.

More and more voices were being raised, calling for an end to a competition described as 'demeaning to women, the council and the resort'. The relationship between Lancaster City Council and the contest had been shaky for some time and after the 1989 final the Council decided to bring it to an end. In the words of the *Morecambe Guardian*, 'The resort's greatest attraction in the Fifties and Sixties has faded and now she is to be jilted'. The title 'Miss GB' was put up for sale.

Pontins expressed an interest but in November 1989 it was announced that businessman Harvey Pritchard, brother of Julia Morley of Mecca, would pay £48,000, determined to transform the "faded bathing beauty cult" into "something relevant to the 1990s". Unfortunately, Mr Pritchard proved to be a less successful businessman than he claimed when it was revealed in February 1991 that he was heavily in debt and the £48,000 had failed to materialise. With no-one else showing any interest, the Council sold the title to Pontins for a mere £10,000. However, Miss GB was finally off its hands.

Both the *Daily Telegraph* and the *Guardian* carried articles reminiscing about the demise of the beauty contest and how, in the 'liberated 1990s', it had become 'old hat, an anachronism of a garish past'. The loss of TV coverage had been the final straw as 'the incidental shots of (chilly and damp) Morecambe had been prized by a council, desperate to keep the resort going in the face of cheap (hot and dry) Spanish holidays'. The newspapers carried quotes from Eileen Blamire, Chair of Lancaster City Council Arts and Events Committee, who stated firmly that they would never stage such a thing again. "We were all so naïve in our twenties and thirties but when women started going on platforms to protest, I started thinking. Those women changed ideas. We woke up and asked ourselves what were we doing, spending time watching women being paraded like this? And then it seemed bygone, outdated and boring. It didn't take a revolution; it was dead and the audience was gone."

Meanwhile, activity had continued on the old swimming pool site with the construction of the new Bubbles indoor pool. Progress was delayed for a while when workmen encountered a five foot thick stone wall, part of the 1930s sea defences and plans had to be amended. Eventually, on Monday 17th July 1989, a little later than expected, the Bubbles 'fun pool' was officially opened by the mayor, Councillor Fred Wilcox, in the company of local schoolchildren and their parents who had been invited to preview the new experience. He believed that Bubbles "marked another step in the regeneration of Morecambe as a major tourist centre". On the following day, according to the *Morecambe Guardian*, the public 'poured through the doors'.

The exterior of Bubbles, seen on a fine spring day from the Promenade Gardens.

Buoyed by this favourable start, the Bubbles development company talked of investing up to £50 million in Morecambe, hoping for contracts to build a marina and shopping and leisure facilities. Unfortunately, despite people being able to use the pool in winter, the early enthusiasm began to wane; attendances started to fall during 1990. Abruptly in February 1991, Bubbles was declared closed – Clifford Barnett Developments had ceased trading. With the site's uncertain future in the hands of the Official Receiver, the Council held emergency meetings to ensure the attraction could open for the summer. Although the budget was strained, both indoor and outdoor pools were able to open and all the events booked for the Superdome went ahead. By September, however, the tourism department was overspent and the decision was taken to close Bubbles for the winter. Keeping the indoor pool going would cost £18,000 per month and it was said that the Council would lose less money if it locked the doors and gave a £10 note to everyone who wanted to go in!

Bubbles was eventually handed over to Lancaster City Council in January 1992, the liquidators having failed to find any private company willing to take over the lease. Worried that it would remain closed for the coming season, hoteliers pleaded for its opening, spurred on by fears of being sued by holidaymakers under the Trade Descriptions Act – Bubbles had appeared in all the resort's advertising and entrance was often included in packages offered by hotels. The Council duly obliged and a greater effort was made to encourage local people to use the pool out of season. In the spring of 1993, the complex was again saved from closure when a private company, Sport and Leisure Management, agreed to take it over but only after the Council had carried out £140,000 worth of repairs.

The newly revamped Bubbles opened in April with bright blues and yellows in the indoor spaces and new changing rooms. Further attractions were added to both pools and the children's play area; the entrance fee was kept at £9 to entice people to stay all day and spend money in the shop, cafés and bars. Financial problems continued to

Described as 'Morecambe's own tropical paradise', the Bubbles indoor pool had a water temperature of 84°F (29°C) and features such as a 60 metre water slide, wild water wave ride, water cannon and bubblers. Seating was provided on the terraces for swimmers and spectators with easy access to the poolside snack bar.

Advertising leaflet for Bubbles.

dog the venture, coming to a head when Lancaster City Council was forced to make a one-off payment of £2.5 million to clear all debts accrued during the original partnership with Clifford Barnett Developments.

Summer 1995 brought some respite with the hot weather drawing in the crowds but, true to form, another cloud loomed on the horizon. On August 11th ambulances queued up outside Bubbles while paramedics carried out coughing, vomiting and crying children with stinging eyes and breathing problems. Chlorine stored in a tank in the basement had leaked and mixed with other chemicals to produce a gas which seeped into the changing rooms. Luckily no serious lasting harm was done and the Council was absolved from blame but the episode dented the pool's popularity.

Attendances steadily declined during the 1997/98 season and the future of Bubbles once again came up for discussion. The current contract was due to run out in April 1999 and the Council was seriously considering its non-renewal. Could the site have another, more profitable use? A public consultation showed that 70% of locals thought Bubbles was important to Morecambe and almost half said they would be willing to contribute up to £5 extra council tax to keep it open. The contract was extended to cover the 1999 season at the end of which it was found that the Bubbles Leisure Group, caretaker of the site, was basically insolvent and owed various creditors £174,000.

Throughout 2000 debate about the future of Bubbles continued, weighing up the costs of keeping it open, possibly mothballing it in hopes of better times ahead or demolishing it as soon as possible. Opinion on the Council was divided, more or less on party lines – the Conservatives were very much in favour of closure while the Morecambe Bay Independents vowed they would do anything to keep it open. Suggestions as to how to afford this included no Christmas lights, no fireworks, not replenishing the beach sand, dismissing Council officers, diverting money from the Salt Ayre sports centre and even a risqué calendar featuring councillors, in very little, in the pool!

One developer wanted to transform Bubbles into a children's leisure complex but required the Council to spend £1.55 million on building work and running costs – needless to say his proposal was turned down. Bubbles was not included in the 2001 holiday brochure. An eleventh hour bid by Kalber Leisure (the erstwhile developers of the Midland Hotel) was scuppered when their financial irregularities came to light and they hastily left the scene. Demolition was decreed and the bulldozers moved in at the end of September 2001. By June 2002 the site was on the market; offers were invited for a 125 year lease for a development which could not be residential, retail, office or industrial.

Morecambe's mixed fortunes persisted through the 1990s and well into the 21st century. The bad times have included the ill-fated Mr Blobby theme park, which cost the Council not only money but a serious loss of face. No summer Illuminations have taken place since 1996. Frontierland closed in 1999, unable to compete with the greater thrills to be experienced just down the coast in Blackpool, leaving Morecambe without a funfair and part of the promenade dominated by supermarkets and a fenced off derelict space. Having put up with this sorry state of affairs for more than twenty years, a group of local artists has used this as a backdrop for a series of murals, with the result that the fence itself has become something of an attraction! The Superdome, spared when the rest of the Leisure Park was demolished in 2001, continued for another ten years before it too met its end.

On the plus side, despite its closure in 2000, the Midland Hotel resisted demolition and was brought back to life by the developers Urban Splash and has become a destination for visitors in its own right. The Winter Gardens is now in the hands of a Preservation Trust able to access grants to help save the iconic building. With the help of a band of volunteers it is gradually being restored as a theatre and arts venue. The disused Promenade station has also been transformed into a space for music and other events. In the West End, the Alhambra has undergone renovation and the housing stock has been significantly improved. On the promenade the simple addition of a statue of one of the resort's favourite sons, Eric Morecambe, has proved a magnet for visitors – including the Queen! Children can still play happily on the sandy beach in Central Morecambe while the sea defences in place elsewhere have greatly reduced the risk of flood damage for those living on or near the front. The enduring popularity of the bird sculptures of the Tern project reflects a re-awakened interest in the natural beauty and wildlife of the bay attracting a different type of visitor. More people are now appreciating the heritage of Morecambe itself. The long-awaited opening of the Bay Gateway link to the M6 (principally to improve access to the port of Heysham) has provided an easier and more direct route to Morecambe, avoiding long delays in congested Lancaster.

The final piece of the jigsaw remains the former home of the Super Swimming Stadium. Parts of the Promenade Gardens have been lost to car parks but the stadium site has remained empty. An attempt to build blocks of flats there in 2012 (despite the Council's strictures in 2002) was met with considerable opposition. Another economic downturn made the project unviable and it failed to gain planning permission. Since then the site has been an arena for temporary fairgrounds, a circus and out-door performances but there has been no permanent structure. Morecambe is holding its breath, anticipating the next great miracle to save its fortunes which, it hopes, will take place on that very site – the proposed Eden Project North.

The newly completed Super Swimming Stadium photographed from the balcony of the Winter Gardens in 1936.

Eighty-five years later, the scene from the same viewpoint in 2021 shows the site vacant and ripe for redevelopment.

THIS OTHER EDEN

NINE

On Monday 31st January 2022, Lancaster City Council approved, unanimously, a planning application by Eden Project International Ltd for a mixed leisure development on 4.6 hectares of Morecambe's Central Promenade, mostly on land once occupied by the Super Swimming Stadium and its successors. Since the opening of its Cornwall site twenty years previously, the Eden Trust has worked to build relationships between people and the natural world with the aim of protecting the planet and encouraging sustainability. Talks began with the Council in 2019 when Morecambe had been chosen for what was hoped to be Eden Project North. Morecambe was selected because of its position on the shores of a bay whose natural environment is held to be of international significance but also because the town had suffered periods of economic and social decline and was deserving of investment for positive change. The cost of the whole enterprise is estimated to be £125 million of which a proportion is already in hand. The realisation of the project by 2024 does depend very much on substantial Government funding which, it is argued, should be forthcoming as part of the promised 'levelling up' agenda for the entire region.

The proposed development will combine a range of indoor and outdoor experiences based on connecting people with Morecambe Bay. Its layout is designed to reflect the neighbouring marine environment; the large buildings will resemble shells and the linking structures echo a dunescape with an undulating 'green roof' topped with a range of coastal vegetation and walls incorporating recycled shells and stones. A new landscaped earth embankment will enclose the actual paid-to-enter attraction but the landscaping will continue beyond the boundary into the areas with free public access. In line with the Eden ethos, the aim is to be a Net-Zero Carbon project.

Among issues raised at the planning meeting, a major concern was the increase in traffic coupled with a lack of parking space. No extra parking is to be made available on the site, with visitors encouraged to use public transport. Those wishing to travel by car will be required to book, along with their timed entrance ticket, a parking slot in an existing Morecambe carpark or at the Park-and-Ride service at Junction 34 of the M6, completing their journey by shuttle bus.

The impact of the development on Morecambe's existing buildings of note also came under discussion. The War Memorial was felt not to be significantly affected because

Artist's impression showing the distribution of the shell structures within their landscaped surroundings.

it already occupied a 'busy spot' and the precise positioning of the shell structures meant that it would still retain its view towards the sea. Similarly, the Winter Gardens would not lose its direct sea view as it would overlook the proposed Rhythm Garden. However, the height of the shells (nearly 37 metres above sea level at maximum) would mean that views of the Midland Hotel from some parts of Morecambe would be restricted and its commanding position on the seaward side of the promenade would be compromised to a certain extent.

Overall, the perceived advantages of the project were considered to greatly outweigh the negative points, with enhanced opportunities for the tourism industry, employment generally and education. Lancaster and Morecambe College is already developing courses in eco-tourism and improving the skill-sets required for the anticipated new jobs. Morecambe is still very much a deprived area and Eden Project North, if successful, could be just the catalyst necessary to spark regeneration.

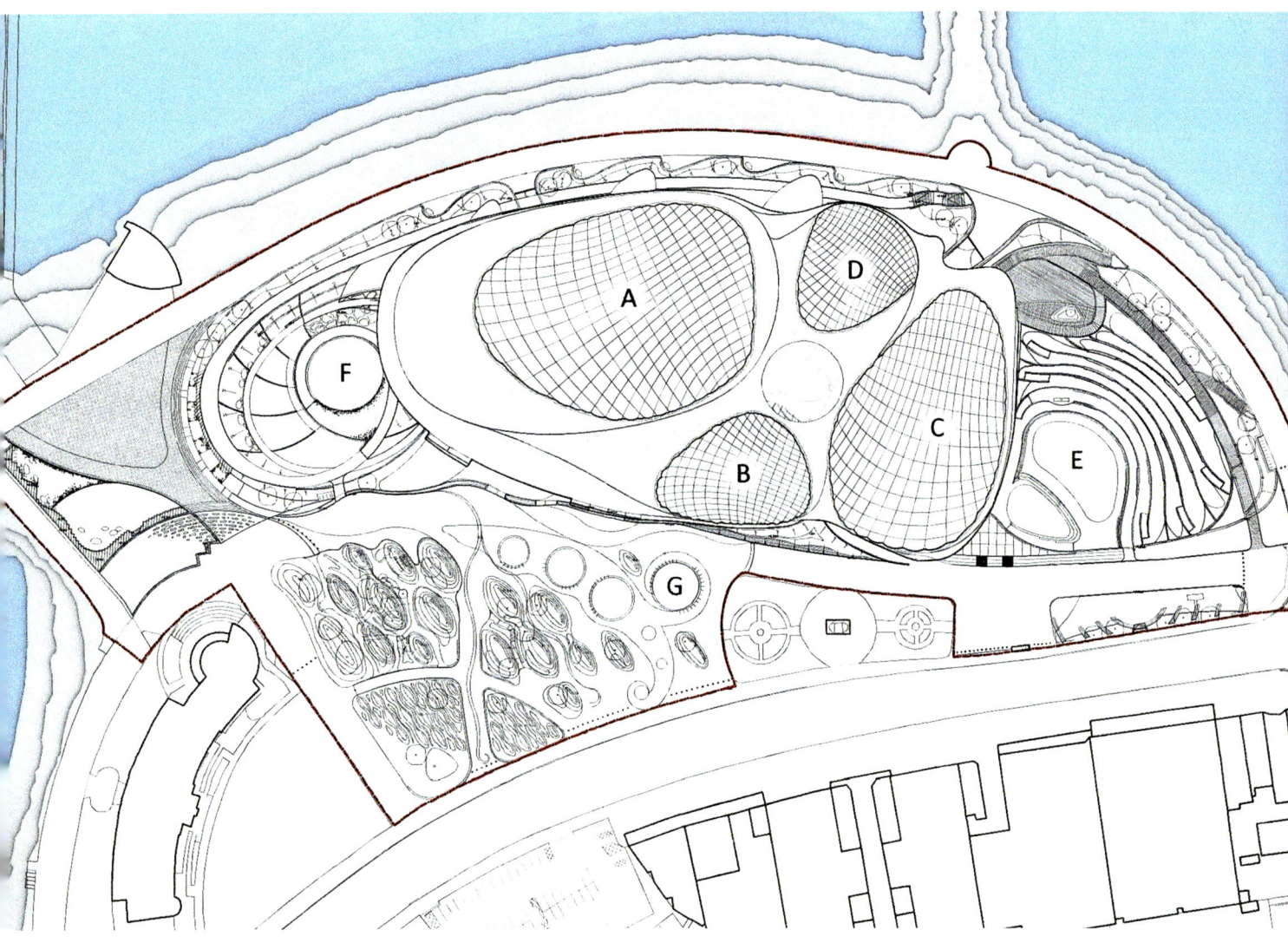

Plan of the site layout. On entering the complex a visitor will have the choice of four very different shell pavilions to explore.

- A   Rhythm Machine: the largest of the buildings will extend over three floors and include plants, art works and immersive theatrical experiences to illustrate the major themes of 'Above and Below the Bay' and rhythms associated with sun, moon and tides.

- B   Bay Hall: will house visitor information and exhibition space at ground level and offices and staff facilities in the basement.

- C   Bay Glade: will provide a landscape focusing on well-being over two floors.

- D   Natural Observatory: will have an observatory on the first floor and space for exhibitions and educational programmes at lower ground level.

Surrounding the buildings will be outdoor gardens designed to reflect the flora and geology of the coastal environment. To the east the Rhythm Garden (E) reimagines the existing Bay Arena and provides a flexible space which can be used for outdoor events in summer, while to the west the beds of the Tide Garden (F) spiral down to a central pool. Located between the four large shells and Marine Road will be seven small cylindrical structures called Energy Pods (G), five metres high, which will house energy related infrastructure and be connected to each other by a canopy fitted with solar panels.

The shell structures are to be made with a lightweight grid covered with ethylene tetrachloroethylene (ETFE) cladding which is energy efficient and can tolerate a wide range of temperature and resist corrosion. Photovoltaic cells will be incorporated for solar power.

Above: Looking towards the proposed Eden North from the shore with the Winter Gardens on the left and Stone Jetty to the right.

Right: An imagined scene inside one of the shell pavilions.

ACKNOWLEDGEMENTS

A book such as this could not have been produced without the help and co-operation of many people. The authors would like to express their gratitude to those organisations and individuals who have kindly given their time and/or have allowed images to be used.

For sharing their memories of the Super Swimming Stadium, particular thanks go to Pete Aspinall, Louie Carrick, Arthur Casson, Trevor Horn, Gillian McDonnell, Sheila Modley, Charlie Overett, Sharman Robinson, Fiona Salter, Roy True and June Wray.

Thanks to David Markson, Jan Baines-Burton and Janet Elliott for biographical details of their fathers, producers of all but two of the Aqua Shows staged at the stadium.

Thanks also to the staff at Morecambe Library, Morecambe Heritage Centre and Lancaster City Museums and to Morecambe Bay Partnership for the loan of recording equipment.

Last but not least, a big thank you to Ivan and Lucy Frontani without whose help and expertise this book would not have been published.

AUTHORS

Barry and Lesley Guise are both retired teachers with an interest in local history. Their previous book, *Portrait of a Village*, is a social history through postcards of Bolton-le-Sands, the village where they live with their two cats, Lyra and Calypso.

BIBLIOGRAPHY

Ayton, Richard & Daniell, William, *A Voyage Round Great Britain* (Longman, 1814-25)

Bingham, Roger, *Lost Resort? The Flow and Ebb of Morecambe* (Cicerone, 1990)

Briggs, Steven & Harris, Diane, *Sun, Fun and Crowds: Seaside Holidays Between the Wars* (Tempus Publishing, 2000)

Cole, Beverley & Durack, Richard, *Railway Posters 1923-1947* (Laurence King, 1992)

Ferry Kathryn, *The British Seaside Holiday* (Shire Publications, 2009)

Gosling, Lucinda, *The British Seaside* (Pen & Sword, 2017)

Gray, Fred, *Designing the Seaside: Architecture, Society and Nature* (Reaktion Books, 2006)

Landreth, Jenny, *Swell: A Waterbiography* (Bloomsbury Sport, 2017)

Parr, Susie, *The Story of Swimming* (Dewi Lewis Media, 2011)

Potter, Terry, *Magnificent Morecambe* (Carnegie, 1989)

Powers, Alan, ed., *Farewell My Lido* (Thirties Society, 1991)

Quick, R.C., *The History of Morecambe and Heysham* (Morecambe Times, 1963)

Shaw, Gareth & Williams, Allan, eds. *The Rise and Fall of British Coastal Resorts* (Pinter, 1997)

Smith, Janet, *Liquid Assets: The Lidos and Open Air Swimming Pools of Britain* (English Heritage, 2005)

Spalding, John, *Poulton-le-Sands: A History of Morecambe* (Unpublished, Morecambe Library, 1974)

Wood, Ghislaine, ed., *Art Deco by the Sea* (Sainsbury Centre for Visual Arts, 2020)

IMAGE CREDITS

Please note that where more than one image appears on a page, each is identified by a letter and sometimes by two letters: T(Top), C(Centre), B(Bottom) and L(Left), R(Right).
Every effort has been made to trace copyright holders.

Libraries, Museums and Archives

Bradford District Museums and Galleries: 54T, 55

Dover Museum: 59

Eden Project: 184, 186T, 186B, 187

Grimshaw and Eden Project: 185

Lancaster City Museums: 9, 13, 14T, 18B, 19B, 21, 24, 36, 40B, 41T, 41B, 47, 56B, 57T, 64T, 69, 73T, 75, 78, 81B, 82T, 82B, 83C, 86T, 86BL, 86BR, 87, 102T, 102B, 103B, 104T, 107T, 111B, 116, 117, 120, 122, 127T, 134TR, 139, 146B, 151

Morecambe Guardian: 163

Morecambe Heritage Centre: 77, 83T, 93B, 95, 96, 105T, 105B, 107B, 126T, 127B, 128, 129, 131T, 131B, 134B, 136, 137, 138, 139, 140, 141T, 141B, 143BR, 145, 149T, 149B, 153, 154, 155T, 156, 157

Morecambe Library: 10, 31, 32, 46, 48, 92, 94BR, 108T, 110, 121B, 130T, 130B, 144T, 170, 172, 174T, 178, 179B

Ordnance Survey: 54B

RIBA: 52

Science Museum Group: 68

The *Visitor*: 27, 33, 42, 49, 106B, 109T, 161L, 161R, 169

Woodfall Films: 135B

Private Individuals

Authors' collection: 3, 11, 12, 14B, 16, 20, 56T, 58, 63B, 65B, 106T, 174B, 181T

David Algar: 19T, 39, 44, 63T, 111T, 118B, 119, 121T, 124T, 124B, 126B, 132, 133, 134TL, 135T, 143TL, 143TR, 143BL

Jan Baines-Burton: 74, 99T

Bridget Belson: 79

Louie Carrick: 83B, 88, 89, 93T, 94TL, 94TR, 94BL, 99TR, 111C

Janet Elliott: 99B

Joseph Hardman: 17

Steven Jefferson: 179T

David Markson: 98

Malcolm O'Neil: 108B

Charlie Overett: 84

Vivienne Pearson: 109C, 109B

Fiona Salter: 61T, 61B

Irene Seddon: 118T, 147

Geoff Shingler: 38, 64B, 65T

Marion Smith: 97, 103T

Robert Speirs: 152

Roy True: 73B, 76, 104B

June Wray: 81T, 90, 91, 150

Front cover image: Authors' collection

Back cover images: Louie Carrick (T), David Algar (C), Morecambe Heritage Centre (B)

INDEX

Aquabats 67, 71-2, 98, **99**, 120
Aquabelles 72, 80, **90**
Aquagoons 72, 76, 80
Aqualoonies 77, 80, **82-3**, 84, 89
Aqualovelies 71-2, 77, 80, **87**, 88-92, **93**, **107**
Aquamaniacs 72
Aqua Shows 71-2, **73**, 74, 76-7, 79-80, **81**, 84-5, **86-7**, 88-9, 92-3, **93-4**, 95, **95**
Art Deco 35, 55
Aspinall, Pete 74, 77, **77**, 80
Ayton, Richard 7

Baines, George 72, 74, 79-80, 90, 98-9, **99**
Band arena 29, 55, 114, 142, 175
Bank holidays 10-11
Bardsley, Sharman 150-2, **152**, 153
Bare pool 13, **13**, 14, **14**, **16**, 17
Bath 5-6
Bath Hotel 11, **11**
Bath Superintendents 164
Bathing attire 8-9, 15, **18-19**, **21**, 36, **36**, 37, **56-7**, 58, **58**, **64**, 106, 113, **116**, 147, **147**
Bathing huts 9-10, 14, 142, 175
Bathing machines 8-9, **9**, **10**, 14
Bathing regulations 8-9, 10, 13
Battery Hill 31, **31**, 32
Bayliss, Pamela **122**, 123
BBC TV 132, 176
Beauty contests 62, 67, 90, 113-157, 171, 175, 177
Big Bender 173, 174, **174**
Blackpool 23, 35, 60, 76, 89, 95, 98, 104, 123, 125, 165, 180
Blake, Perry **78**, 79, **79**
Blower, Tom 19, **19**
Blue Seagull 109, **109**
Bournemouth 72, 74, 76, 90, 98
Bowers, Johnny 72, **76**
Bradford 8, 21, 43
Briggs, Edwin 113, 114
Brighton 6-7
Bubbles 173, 177, 178, **178**, 179, **179**, 180

Buckle, Claude 69
Butlins 125, 132, 136

Campbell Cooper, George 80, 84-5, 88, 91-2, 95, 99, **99**, 164
Carrick, Louie 88-9, **88-9**, 93
Carter, Ray 85, **89**, 95
Cascade 106, **106-7**
Crazy golf 55, 111, ***111***
Cross, Kenneth 24-5, 33
Cross & Sutton 24-6, 31, 37-8
Crystal Hall 28-9, 31
Curtiss, Johnny 76

Daily Dispatch 62, 113
Daily Herald 125
Daily Mail 51, 114
Daily Telegraph 177
Daly, Charles 19, *19*
Dawne, Doreen **126**
Digby, Everard 5
Diving 45, 51-2, 58, 60, **61**, 67, 71-2, **75**, 76-7, **78**, 79, 95, 104, **104**, 114, 120
Drummond, Mary 114, **116**
Dunster, Jean 114, **116**, **119**

Eade, Charles 113-14, 117, **119**, 123, 125, **126**, 128
Eden Project North 181, 183-6, **184-7**
English Channel 11, 15-17, 20, 59
Entertainer, The 135, **135**
Eugène Mermaids 59, **59**

Fahy, F.C. 8-9, 33, 45
Farey, Cyril 24
Fisher, Dorothy 114, 129, **129**, 137, 152-7, **155-7**
Fishermen/Pilots 14, 15-16, **18**, 20
Flook, Leonard 42, **42**, 60, 66, 164
Floyer, John 6
Formby, George 117, **119**, **126**
Forsberg, Gerald 17, 20, **20**
Foundation stone 33, **33**
Fransen, Roy 72, 79-80, 98-9, **99**
Fyfe, Ron **93**

Gay Steppers 93, 105, **105**
Gibson, Swede 74, 80, **84**, **104**
Goya 136
Grange-over-Sands 15, 17, **17-18**, 20, 35, 165
Great Yarmouth 79, 99
Guardian, The 177
Gurley, Jennifer **156**
Gynt, Greta 123

Harrogate 6, 24
Health and fitness 5-7, 10, 12, 20, 23, 25, 36-7, 45, 51-2, 66
Heating 51, 53, 60, 66, 171, 179
Hellewell, Peter 85, **89**
Hill, Oliver 37, 55
Horn, Trevor 95, 104

Illuminations 62, **63**, 180

Judges 114-17, **118-19**, **121-2**, 123, **124**, 144-5, **146**, **148**, 176

Kirkham, Wendy 72, 74, 90, **90**
Kursaal 20, 28

Lambert, Jack **104**
Lancaster 7-8, 10, 14, 168, 180
Lashbrook, Ed 85, **89**, **93**, 95
Laurel & Hardy 121, **121**
Law, Brierley 16
Leisure Park 159-60, 162, 167, **169**, 170, **170**, 171, **172**, 173, **174**, 175-6, 180
Lidos 23-4, 35-6, **36**, 37, 165
Lindsay Parkinson & Sons 32-3, 38, 160
LMS Railway 26, 28, 37, 43, 45, 68

Mackintosh bathing 10
Marco, Leon 71-2, 74, 76, 80, 90, 98, **98**, 114
Martin, Jackie, 72, 74, 80
Martin, Malcolm 60, 61, **61**
Mayo, Christine **133**, **156**
McGaffigan, Sheila 150, **151**, 152-3

191

Mecca 123, 125, 132, 136, 177
Mee, Brenda *146*, *156*
Midland Hotel 26, 28, 37, 39, *41*, 43, *44*, 55, 140, 152, 180, 184
Midnight bathing 64, *64-5*
Ministry of Health 29, 31
Miss Great Britain 67, 88-9, 93, 95, 123-157, 171, 175, 177
Mitchell, June 123
Modernism 35, 37-9
Morecambe, growth of 7-8, 21
Morecambe, decline of 168-9, 175
Morecambe Bay 7-8, 13, 20, 35
Morecambe & Wise *126*, *145*, 180
Morley, Eric 123, 125, 132
Morris, Don 80, *84*, 85, *89*, 91
Munlack, Jimmy 72, *76*

Netzell, Mildred 71-2, *73*
New Brighton 35, 51, 165

Old Harbour 26, *27*, 29, 30
Old Harbour Committee 28, 31, 33, 45
Olympic Games 17, 59, 79, 89
Ormes, Yvonne *137*, *152*
Overett, Charlie 17, 84, *84*

Parliamentary Bill 26
Paterson, Bill 85, *89*, *93*
Payne, Jack & Hammer, Will 72, 74
Perkins, Dorothy 17, 20
Pinder, Edward 92, 164
Pontins 76, 95, 136, 175, 177
Pretty, Violet 124, *124*, 125, *134*, *157*
Pryce, Elaine 123, *124*
Public baths 10-12, *12*, 110

Railways 8, 11, 68-9, 168
Railway posters 37, 68-9, *68-9*
Reid, Lydia 113, 116, *116*, 117, *117*, *145*
Remedial Department 52, 110, *110*
Rennie, Michael 115-16
RIBA 24-5
Rivers, June 114, *116*, 117, *119*, 148
Robinson, Elizabeth *156*
Rodgers, Ray 72
Rollier, Auguste 35
Romans 5
Roper, Doreen 114, *116*
Royalty 5-7, 180
Russell, Richard 6

Sandylands 15, 20
Savage, R.B. 28
Scarborough 6, 76
Sea bathing 8-9
Sea wall 29, 31-2, *32*
Sherwin, Frank 69
Shipbreaking 26-7
Shiverers Club 109
Slade, Betty 72
Smith, Ambrose 71, 114
Smith, Eric & Eve 85, *95*, 95
Smith, Glynn 92, 95-7, 109
Southport 35, 45, 79, 89, 95, 125, 165
Spas 6, 20-21
Spink, Gay *141*, *156*
Stamp, Josiah 43-5
Stearne, William 15-16
Stone Jetty 28-9, 32
Sunbathing 28-9, 35-6, *36*, 95
Sunday Dispatch 113-14, 117, 123, 125, 132

Superdome 171, *172*, 173, *174*, 175-6, 180
Super Swimming Stadium:
  construction 38-42, *39-41*
  opening 43-5, *44*, *46-7*
  description 51-52, 54-7, *54-7*, 96-7, *102-3*
  closure 97-8, 142, 159-165
  demolition 164, *165*
Sutton, Cecil 25, 33

Taylor, Gillian 150-2, *152*, 154, *154*, 156, *156*
Thompson, Don 96, *96*, 105
Tolley, Alice 115, *116*
Trampoline 85, 105, *105*,

Victoria Swimming Club 11, 13-14

Walker, Norman 164
Walsh, Roy 79, *79*, *93*, 95
Ward, T.W. 26
Webb, Matthew 11
Westbury, Diane *136*
West End Swimming Club 11
Williams, Leila 132, *132*
Windsor Water Woollies 58, *58*, *106*, 113, 115, 120
Winstanley, Kathleen 140, *140*
Winter Gardens 11, *12*, 15, 23-4, 41, 90, 114, 116, 139, *139*, 142, 168, 175, 180, 184
Wittie, Robert 6
World War Two 60, 62, 66, 115, 120
Wray, June 74, 85, *89*, 90-1, *90-1*, *93*, 96, 150, *150*, 151-2

Yorkshire TV 137-8, 175-6